South End Boy

South End Boy

Growing up in Halifax in the tumultuous '30s and '40s

Jim Bennet

Formac Publishing Company Limited
Halifax

Formac Publishing Company Limited recognizes the support of the Province of Nova Scotia through Film and Creative Industries Nova Scotia. We are pleased to work in partnership with the Province of Nova Scotia to develop and promote our creative industries for the benefit of all Nova Scotians. We acknowledge the support of the Canada Council for the Arts which last year invested $157 million to bring the arts to Canadians throughout the country.

Cover design: Tyler Cleroux
Cover image: Courtesy of Jim Bennet

Library and Archives Canada Cataloguing in Publication
Bennet, Jim, 1931-, author
    South End boy : growing up in Halifax in the tumultuous '30s and '40s / Jim Bennet.

Issued in print and electronic formats.
ISBN 978-1-4595-0389-2 (bound).--ISBN 978-1-4595-0390-8 (epub)

    1. Bennet, Jim, 1931- --Childhood and youth. 2. Lyricists--Nova Scotia--Biography. 3. Authors--Nova Scotia--Biography. 4. Halifax (N.S.)--Biography. I. Title.

FC2346.26.B46A3 2015   971.6'22503   C2015-903531-7
                                                    C2015-903532-5

Formac Publishing Company Limited
5502 Atlantic Street
Halifax, Nova Scotia, Canada
B3H 1G4
www.formac.ca

Printed and bound in Canada.

In memory of my parents, Helene Sandford Bennet and Charles Lindsay Bennet.

My beautiful mother as a newlywed.

My father, the ANZAC sergeant, World War I.

Contents

Preface

THIS BOOK IS ABOUT HALIFAX, Nova Scotia, the city in which my young friends and I were lucky enough to grow up. Our boyhood spanned the Great Depression and World War II. Looking back on those years, the thing that amazes me most is that while girls — like my younger sisters Jane and Caroline — led a rather sheltered life, boys like me were given a pretty free rein. Once the first five or six years went by, we had leave to wander, explore and survey all over the South End. As long as we were home for dinner (now, in general parlance, lunch) supper (now dinner), and bed (we had a strict bedtime), we could consider the streets, alleys, open spaces and even public buildings our turf. And, in the safer community of that time, nobody worried much about it. The seashore, the railway tracks, the ponds and parks, the transit system, the Commons, the Citadel: these and other attractions formed a rich and instructive playground.

The Halifax of my youth was not a colourful town. Rather, it was quite drab — a place where the homes were painted brown, grey or, less commonly, white. City planning was not a very advanced discipline, which meant that in some areas there were gas stations, Chinese laundries and even a decrepit arena right next to handsome homes. There were swaths of untidy brush, thick woods (Dalhousie, Marlborough, Point Pleasant) and scattered vacant lots.

The North Commons was a flat desert of grit and gravel with struggling plantain weeds as the only sign of vegetation.

With the beginning of World War II, barracks and prefabricated homes sprang up seemingly overnight; uniforms became as common as "civvies." But we lucky lads (too young for service and only faintly aware of the carnage happening in the war zones to people only a few years older) adventurously roamed the town and made our own fun. Even now I sometimes look back on my youth with mixed feelings: a combination of guilt and gratitude.

Now, at an age at which short term memory too often diminishes, my cherished recollections of boyhood are surprisingly intact. My theory is that one retains a stronger recall of original experiences than of subsequent, oft-repeated ones. In any event, the remembered Halifax in which these "firsts" in life took place is a rich landscape that I feel compelled to share with readers who, I hope, love the old city as I do.

1

Home

THE HOUSE I GREW UP in, at the corner of South and Dalhousie Streets, was built in the midtwenties, a few years before I was born. It's a solid, four-square, two-storey home, originally built for a wealthy South End lady and the English military officer she had married. The marriage didn't work out, and the house was put up for sale. My father, before his marriage, had been rooming or boarding in various places near Dalhousie University, where he taught. He secured a mortgage and bought it as a family home.

The place was obviously built for people of some privilege. It had an entrance hall, large living and dining rooms, a kitchen and butler's pantry on the main floor and an open sun porch off the dining room. Upstairs were the master bedroom, complete with fireplace; a dressing room with large closet (later to become my childhood bedroom); a guest bedroom; a den and a maid's room. In the early 1930s there was an underground municipal gas line running along South Street that fed the kitchen stove and a "Ruud" brand jacket water heater in the cellar. Like most homes of the day, heat came from a coal furnace. Coal was delivered

My home, when Dalhousie Street was still a dirt track.

in horse-drawn, two-wheeled wagons, and tipped down a chute through a cellar window into the coal room.

The furnace virtually ruled the house, presenting a series of daunting daily chores. Last thing before my father's bedtime, it had to be stoked by shovel with enough coal to last the night. It would be down to a dull glow by breakfast time, and each week a solidified mass of coal residue, called clinker, had to be pried out of the furnace with a long iron bar and shovelled into a metal garbage can to be collected as part of the weekly garbage removal. The process sent a ferocious clanking sound throughout the house, transmitted via the pipes of the heating system. Then the shovel had to be put to use again as the furnace was restoked and relit, keeping the hot-water radiators warm until the next shovelling session. The arrangement worked by judgment, estimation and hard work alone: no thermostats, no igniters, no alarms, no respite. The penalty for inattention was panic: pipes could freeze, burst and flood the place. The house would go cold and plumbers with blowtorches would have to be summoned, as the family huddled under blankets.

The only pleasure my father ever found in that tyrannical furnace came when, on the occasional morning, he would take a couple of smoked herring (kippers) and a toasting rack to the cellar and broil his favourite seafood over the coals for his breakfast.

There were other labour-inducing deficiencies in the design of the house. At the top of the concrete foundation, only a row of uninsulated cedar shingles kept the winter cold at bay. Incredibly, in those days of rudimentary building codes, there was no door to the outside from the cellar. The only form of exit was a window through which my poor father had to wrestle the garbage and ash cans. He tried to insulate the heating pipes by tying thick layers of student test papers around them, a solution that proved quite unsatisfactory. Luckily, my maternal grandfather William Sandford was a stonemason and plasterer living on nearby Walnut Street. He carefully bricked in the top of the foundation and cut a door into its side so that ashes, garbage and firewood could be dealt with. He also created a masonry garage under the sun porch to house our first family car, a 1940 Studebaker.

If my father had to put a lot of work into chores associated with heating, other household tasks were equally demanding. Food was kept cool in an icebox, requiring large blocks of ice delivered to the back door. We had no washing machine during the thirties. The wash was done in a set-tub and wrung out with a hand-cranked wringer, then hung out on a clothesline that ran between the sun porch and a tall post at the foot of the garden. Detergents had not yet been invented, and everything but the family was washed using Surprise Soap. Even dishes were washed by hand, using a small, long-handled wire cage filled with scraps of leftover laundry soap. The sewing machine wasn't electrified, but had a foot-operated treadle. Carpets were cleaned every spring by hanging them up outdoors and whacking them with an implement called a carpet beater. A refrigerator, an electric stove, a radio, a phonograph and a washing machine were gradually acquired sometime during my grade-school days, and each was a cause for celebration!

It's important to note that despite all the work involved and the lack of amenities that today are taken for granted, our house was less demanding than the average family home of the time. Central heating was more comfortable than the coal-burning stove that was the sole source of heat in many modest houses. During part of my childhood, we had a live-in maid, which allowed my mother to put in countless hours typing, proofreading and filing my father's manuscripts. (He was the editor of a set of English school textbooks, the *Canada Books of Prose and Verse*, published by Ryerson.)

The house was regularly transformed into a theatre during the college year as a result of a course my father taught: the History of Drama, English 9. The elective course was obviously much loved by those who took it. It involved presentations of plays, with the characters in full makeshift costumes. Bed sheets served as togas, garbage can lids as shields and fireplace pokers as swords. Though the parts were not fully memorized and the actors read most of the dialogue, the evening dramas were great fun. The living room became the stage, with my mother and others not

Me, age three, with my granny, Millicent Sandford.

involved with a given play seated in the adjoining dining room as the audience. Sometimes we kids were permitted a front seat, sometimes not. My mother would serve sandwiches and coffee after the "production." It was such memorable fun that for years afterward, older people would recognize me as the goggle-eyed boy in the front row and tell me that English 9 was the highlight of their college days.

Today, 1191 Dalhousie Street still looks a comfortable and welcoming place. And if the present inhabitants were to look at a small, square wooden insert in the middle of the dining room floor, they might wonder what had been there when the place was new. I could tell them that it once was the site of a small electric button that, when pressed by the toe of the lady of the house, rang a bell in the kitchen to summon the maid. Once the

My grampy could fix anything.

officer and his disaffected bride moved out, it was used only as a plaything (principally by me). In fact I eventually wore it out. My grandfather was called upon to remove it and replace it with a small, neat, hardwood plug.

In passing the old place on occasion, I take some pleasure in knowing that this little repair, like some bigger ones of brick and mortar, remain in the place as a reminder of my beloved stonemason "Grampy," William Benjamin Sandford.

2

Sounds

WHEN I BEGIN TO DREDGE my mind for memories of the Halifax of my boyhood, I am able to vividly recall the sounds of the place. Sadly, many of them have disappeared from the soundscape of today. Perhaps the most indelible recollection is the noise of the trains from the railway that cut through the city a block from our house. The train noises were particularly welcome as I was tucked into bed. There was nothing more soporific or comforting than the chuff-chuff of a slow freight outbound from the rail yards by the harbour front. It took miles for a loaded freight train to get up to speed, and an engineer's hand had to be sure and responsive if he was to keep the wheels from spinning as he accelerated. When that happened, the chuffing speeded up, producing a variant more like a hurried ch-ch-ch-ch until the steam was throttled back. All children knew this was a black mark against the engineer, because spinning drive wheels tended to cause uneven spots on the rails.

The steam whistles of the passing trains were a child's delight as well. Unlike the unmusical, single-note screech of factory whistles, trains played a chord (always a minor key, creating a wistful, melancholy effect). Even as a kid, I was aware of the subtle variations in pitch, dynamics and duration that could be produced in a given whistle signal, but didn't learn until much later that many engineers of the day had their own signature style, creating a wail that was all their own.

Another well-loved bedtime lullaby was the sound of fog-horns on murky nights. The most comforting were the diaphone signals of major lighthouses, so called because they emitted a low-frequency groan that trailed off with an even lower note (more of a grunt). These could be heard for many miles. Regular harbour traffic produced a symphony of ships' whistles, especially when large vessels were docking or clearing. Communication between tugs and the ship they were assisting was done, in those days, through the exchange of whistle blasts rather than ship-to-ship radio. A large liner would emit a pattern of shuddering blasts giving a particular command: a nudge to starboard, a pull to port. The tug or tugs would reply in their high-pitched way, as children in bed imagined the intricate manoeuvres involved. When the job was accomplished, ship and tug would blow a cheery "ta-ta" as a signoff.

During wartime, naval vessels provided a unique sound: something more like a giant, ear-piercing slide whistle, usually blown in a series of several rising whoops. It's a sound that disappeared from the sonic scene of Halifax not long after the war.

A distinct contribution of World War II fliers to the sound palette of Halifax was the Harvard trainer, a single-engined monoplane used by member nations of the British Commonwealth Air Training Plan. Lads of the time studied aircraft recognition playing cards with more enthusiasm than was usually wasted on schoolwork. They'd compete to see who could identify the most plane silhouettes, both friendly and enemy, as they were dealt. But the yellow Harvard, with its many-paned "greenhouse" cockpit canopy, was so familiar that it didn't even warrant a point. It seemed there was always at least one overhead during daylight hours, and the coarse, droning Harvard sound didn't even prompt us to crane our necks.

Automobiles of the time also had their spectrum of sounds. Many ancient clunkers were nursed through the shortages of wartime until factories retooled for civilian production. (We could recognize a score of makes now disappeared from our streets.) Some passing jalopies were so old they had the old-fashioned Klaxon horn, the one that went "ah-ooo-ga" instead of "beep." Some of us fancied we could identify one or more makes by their engine sound alone (I could do Fords fairly accurately). All were standard shift, of course, and faulty clutching would result in a clashing of gears that set your teeth on edge. In wintertime, passing cars with tire chains gave forth a rhythmic clanging as loose links slapped the insides of the fenders. Backfires, too, were common in the days of more primitive timing mechanism and gas mixture technology. A really good one could burst a car's muffler asunder in a literal flash.

Many other South End sounds could be heard without leaving the house. On Saturdays, the clink of heavy brass rings would drift from the Studley Quoit Club across the street from our house. Peaceful Sunday morning chimes rang out from St. Augustine's Anglican Church in Jollimore village. Rusty clothesline pulleys would squeak on washday (always observed on Monday). And on any day of the week, if the wind was just right, twelve

21

HANG THIS CARD WHERE EVERYONE CAN SEE IT!			

AIR RAID INSTRUCTIONS

When There's A Sneak Attack And **NO WARNING**		When You Hear The Sirens Sound A **WARNING**
Get away from windows and under bed or table. Cover exposed parts of the body.	**AT HOME**	Go to previously selected shelter - preferably in the basement. Keep Radio ON.
Get away from windows or glass doors, and under desk, table or bench. Cover exposed parts of body.	**AT WORK**	Go to previously appointed shelter. Obey instructions of Building Control Director or Post Warden.
Get in any shelter if near to you If no shelter within a few steps, fall flat on your stomach and cover face and eyes with arms.	**ON STREET**	Go to nearest shelter or public building. Keep away from glass. Obey the Wardens.
PULL INTO THE CURB. Turn off ignition. Cover face and eyes and lie on the floor.	**IN VEHICLE**	PULL INTO THE CURB. Turn off ignition. Go to nearest shelter. Keep away from glass. Obey the Wardens.
If your Children are at school, YOU stay where you are. Teachers are trained to look after students.	**CHILDREN AT SCHOOL**	If your Children are at school, YOU stay where you are. Teachers are trained to look after students.

DON'T { LOSE YOUR HEAD . . . .
. START RUMOURS . . .
. . . USE THE TELEPHONE.

AFTER AN ATTACK

1. **Keep calm and follow instructions.**
2. **Don't use Food or Water except from CLOSED containers.**
3. **Join Self-Help Parties under the Wardens.**

— CIVIL DEFENCE HEADQUARTERS, HALIFAX, N. S. —

This hung in our kitchen for five years.

o'clock was announced by the thud of the noonday gun from Citadel Hill.

3

Smells

AIR POLLUTION WAS PERVASIVE ENOUGH in the Halifax of my boyhood to be regarded as simply a fact of life. Consider the numerous sources of coal smoke: virtually every dwelling burned the stuff.

Some people burned hard coal, some the sootier soft coal, and some used coke, which was partially burned coal previously roasted in the manufacture of steel or coal gas. Local industry, steam ships, steam rollers and coal-burning locomotives also added their share to the miasma. The resultant pall that hung over the city, especially in winter, smelled like nothing else: acrid, bitter and chemical. By comparison, wood smoke — at least to those of us who breathed the urban air of the 1930s — is sweet and pleasant.

There were other foul smells, though none quite so virulent, among the assortment remembered from my childhood. One of them visited only when conditions were right; on such occasions, my mother would wrinkle her nose immediately on leaving the house and exclaim, "Oh. . .east wind!" When I first asked how she could tell, she explained that the Imperial Oil refinery on the Dartmouth side of the harbour was precisely due east of our neighbourhood, and even a moderate wind from that direction would bear the gassy pong of hydrocarbons. It was a match for sauerkraut-generated flatus with a note of rotten eggs, and it collected in the sinuses to ill effect.

Keith's Brewery, too, used to waft an awful whiff to the westward when they dumped the spent, reeking grain from the beer-making process. It took me half my childhood to learn exactly what caused the vomitous stench from across the peninsula. Strangely, my loathing of the waste product did nothing to deter my adult fondness for the beverage that gave rise to it.

Roofing or pavement patching meant the smell of hot tar, which children found attractive. The stuff wasn't unique to Halifax, of course, but I count it as a Halifax smell because the city had (and has) so many of the flat-roofed dwellings that depend on tar and gravel for keeping the weather at bay. Great, shiny, lumps of the stuff were melted down by the blowtorch-like burner towed behind the crew's truck. The "reward" for hanging about and awaiting an opportunity to snitch a small gobbet of warm tar was the dubious pleasure of chewing on it. That's right. . .creosote, benzene, toluene and all. Maybe our survival is due to the fact that we spat generously and often. I sincerely hope that in this respect today's youngsters are less idiotic than that generation of long ago.

There's another scent that (though it too could be found the world over) I associate with three major Halifax hospital buildings. These were the original Victoria General (VG), the Halifax Infirmary in its Queen Street incarnation and the old Cogswell Street Military Hospital between Gottingen and Brunswick (where the Staples parking garage now stands). The military institution was like something left over from the time of the Crimean

Carbolic Central: the Victoria General Hospital.

War, the VG an outmoded relic of the Queen after whom it was named, and the Infirmary was neat and modern, with a bit of an art deco flair. What they had in common was the pervasive smell of a common antiseptic, carbolic acid, that sweetish chemical miasma universally known as hospital smell.

The first hospital visit I ever made, at about the age of seven, was to the Cogswell Street institution. My grandfather had taken me for a walk around Citadel Hill one Sunday, and afterwards we descended to street level and visited the ward where an old friend of his lay ill. The long room was lined with dozens of patients in white iron beds. We weren't there long, but the scene and the reek were sufficient to disturb me for a long time afterward.

I also associate the carbolic smell with the Pavilion wing of the Victoria General where my grandfather himself died a few years later. I remember my mother, during her father's illness, rummaging for carfare in her purse as we waited for a tram. Among the contents I noticed a medicine bottle filled with a dark liquid. My curiosity aroused, I asked what it was. Immediately she blushed, and tucked the bottle deeper in the purse. "It's for your grandfather," she replied, obviously uncomfortable. Not to be put off, I persisted. "But what *is* it?" For a moment it seemed she was going to ignore the question. Then, *sotto voce*, she said quickly, "It's a bit of Demerara Rum." Belatedly, I understood. My poor Grampy, sick and near death in a crowded, smelly ward, wanted the small comfort of a drink. And as much as my mother loathed the thought of becoming what was, in her eyes, next thing to a bootlegger, she was going to see that he got it.

The carbolic acid stench signified sickness in my mind until I was grown and the chemical ceased to be used to the extent it once was. I think my mother felt the same way, because the then popular Lifebuoy Soap smelled of carbolic, and she wouldn't have it in our house. (We often had resort to Packer's Pine Tar Soap, reputedly good for the scalp, which sent me off to school smelling like a freshly paved road.)

Mind you, the smells of my boyhood were by no means all harsh and disagreeable. I learned to love the smell of green tomato chow (never a staple in our house) before I ever tasted it. On Saturday mornings in the fall, when I delivered the *Star Weekly* to customers on my route, the spicy-sweet aroma would meet me at every other door and make the job a pleasure. As a bonus, there was the satisfying smell of fresh printer's ink from the glossy new edition. Then there was the wonderful aroma of roasting coffee which emanated from the Java Blend premises on Hollis Street. The proprietor's name was Mr. Sederis, but we knew him affectionately among ourselves as "Coffee Joe." We'd detour a block or two when downtown, just to inhale a satisfying sniff.

A signal of early June (more to the point, the end of school) was the musky, slightly punky scent of newly blossomed hawthorn that pervaded my part of the South End. A walk along Shirley Street would yield the fragrance of fresh-baked bread from Ben's Bakery. Moirs Chocolate Factory scented the entire Grand Parade with its product, while the National Fish plant on the waterfront contributed a bouquet that, when merged with the salt of the North Atlantic, permeated the downtown. I've cherished it all my life as the smell of home.

4

Stores

ONE OF THE THINGS THAT has been lost since my youth is the individuality of stores. These days, one chain grocery or convenience store is much like any other. The small Halifax stores of the thirties had character. They had essential differences, one from another. There were hundreds of them, enough that every neighbourhood had several within a few minutes' walk. Many of them offered credit, and the mutual trust was such that a child could be sent to fetch some household need, say, "Mum says to put it on the bill," and take the purchase home.

In my opinion, Mr. Morris Green of Studley Grocery (corner of Coburg and LeMarchant) could take credit for the greatest assortment of now-vanished delights in the vast confectionery field. Busy and hard-working man that he was, Mr. Green had remarkable patience with the youngsters who pressed their noses against the glass front of his counter, trying to make up their minds. At a penny apiece, there were hard hats, spearmint leaves, honeymoons, liquorice babies, bull's eyes, cinnamon red hots, maple buds, wax lips, BB Bats, jaw breakers, peppermint pillows, Boston baked beans and wax pop bottles full of sweet, coloured water of uncertain provenance. For a nickel, a kid could choose from among such chocolate bars as Denver Sandwich, the Bordeaux Bar (with a dental cavity in every brown-sugary bite), the chewy Eat-More bar full of peanuts and filling-pulling toffee, Smiles and Chuckles and Pal-o-Mine, now all out of favour.

Mr. Green's patience wasn't quite inexhaustible. After four or five minutes of waiting, as a potential buyer shifted from one foot to another in a panic of decision making, there was a gentle mantra he'd use to let us know the clock was running out. It went, "Kamonka monka monka monka mon, boy." Of course that only upped the pressure and forced a too quick decision. Often one left with malted milk balls when a better choice would have been sugar cones.

Mr. Green's establishment was, for the most part, a grocery store. A large stalk of bananas always hung near the entrance and was given a wide berth by kids who knew through the schoolyard grapevine that every bunch concealed at least one deadly, hairy "banana bug" (i.e., tarantula). Shelves full of cans and boxes went to the ceiling. The higher items would be retrieved by the clerk, using a hooked pole to topple tins and cereal boxes which were then deftly caught in one hand. Heavier items were fetched with a long-handled tong-like arrangement. Wedges were cut to order from a big wheel of cheddar. Peanut butter was available in bulk as well as by the jar. Meat was ground to order, with my mother's usual request (relayed by me on errands from home) being the euphonious-sounding "one pound of ground round."

But the Studley Grocery's location, a short block away from both LeMarchant and St. Thomas Aquinas schools, assured it of a steady stream of grade-school candy customers. I like to think that my pennies played a part in the higher education of Mr.

Green's young family. Two of them became physicians and another two became lawyers. One of the latter, Nathan, became the first Jewish Chief Judge of the Nova Scotia Provincial Court, and has a downtown square near the Halifax waterfront named after him. Never underestimate the power of a penny.

Another store near my school was Lipton's at the southeast corner of Jubilee and Walnut. In addition to their candies, the Liptons kept a good stock of novelties from Japan, including cheap paper fans, tin wind-up toys and glass pens filled with useless, coloured "ink." As I recall, the Liptons were also among those who kept a punch board behind the counter. These were pieces of thick fibreboard, drilled with rows of holes, each containing a rolled up slip printed with a winning (or, much likelier, losing) number. Both sides were then pasted over with printed paper showing where the holes lay underneath. A "p" shaped metal puncher hung from the board by a string. You paid your nickel, selected an unused spot, pushed the leg of the implement into it, withdrew the tiny scroll, read it, and (inwardly) wept. I never played this mug's game more than a few times. A nickel spent on candy, though, was a sure winner.

Then there was Levy's at the corner of South and Oxford. Percy Levy and his wife, Gertie, kept what was known as an ice cream parlour (with orange pineapple and maple walnut among my preferences). But they also sold sundries of all kinds, notably tobacco. Among the then popular brands of cigarettes were Sweet Caporal, Winchester, Old Gold, Buckingham, Black Cat, Gold Flake, Craven "A" and Turret. The latter was the Canadian equivalent of the British Woodbines or the French Gauloise: a cheap, blue-collar brand that was available in small nickel packs of five, as well as the full pack of twenty. Better brands were also available in a shallow rectangular tin of fifty, a favourite gift to smokers, known as a "flat fifty."

Chewing tobacco was in wide use, with Shamrock and Club among the leading brands. A native Nova Scotian product was Pictou Twist, sold in the form of a rope of molasses-treated tobacco several inches long. What was chewed had to be spat, and splotches of brown guck (sorry about this) were as common on Halifax sidewalks as chewing gum blots are today. The popularity of chewing tobacco was echoed in the candy available to kids, who could buy plugs of liquorice "chewing tobacco" complete with little lithographed tin brand tags pressed into their surface, just like the real thing. Pipe tobacco was available in small, oval or large, colourful tins. Half and Half, Picobac ("The Pick of Tobaccos") and Old Chum were always on prominent display. One brand, Prince Albert, gave rise to a common telephone prank. "Do you keep Prince Albert in a tin?" "Yes, we do." "Well, let him out!" Gales of laughter followed, and a quick hang up.

Another neighbourhood Ma and Pa store was Bellefontaine's on South Street near Waterloo. The Bellefontaines (always Bell Fountains to us) were a Chezzetcook couple. He sported a magnificent white handlebar moustache. She didn't. I can't swear to this, never having tried it, but word on the street was that if you went to the back door on Sunday (when all groceries were closed by law) and knocked the right knock, they'd sell you a clandestine loaf of bread or quart of milk.

Another well-remembered store was run by Mrs. Al-Molky at the corner of Cogswell and North Park. Not exactly in our neighbourhood, but a habitual stop for some of us who were army cadets of the LeMarchant Street School company. Our Friday afternoon courses at the Armouries took us past this tiny

War Bonds advertising was everywhere.

basement shop, and we'd always pop in for a bracer of Orange
Crush or Lime Rickey. This kind lady obviously enjoyed her
weekly visit by adolescents in uniform, and she welcomed us
warmly. I recall how eager to chat she was, and, in particular, her
nostalgic ramblings about her beloved native land of Lebanon
and how dearly she'd love to visit it once more. A time or two she
came to tears telling us about the mountains of home and of the
beautiful cedars that were the national emblem of that faraway
country. We were somewhat embarrassed but also moved by her
emotiveness, which came as an early lesson in what kind of feelings could come to immigrants, and how our city was evolving.

Though the building is still there, the door to that small, rather
dark little store has been cemented up for years. Bell Fountain's
went the convenience chain route. Levy's little one-storey structure gave way to an apartment building, as did Lipton's. And
the Studley Grocery went from Mr. Green's ownership into the
hands of Bill Mason, then became a pharmacy followed by a

Cadet Bennet and the family dog Pat.

succession of convenience stores, none of them overseen by an aproned proprietor or featuring a stalk of bananas with a curved knife stuck in its stump end.

The thing that sticks in my mind is that every one of the scores of old family corner stores in Halifax provided people of my generation with similar, but by no means identical memories. How lasting those memories can be is confirmed by the fact that the corner of Cogswell and North Park still reminds me of the cedars of Lebanon. And when passing through Coburg and LeMarchant I can still hear, in some recess of my mind, an accented voice gently saying, "Kamonka monka monka monka mon, boy."

5

Eats

PRE–WORLD WAR II HALIFAX WAS not a place of gastronomic opulence, at least in my experience. Whether the grandees of the deep South End devoured frogs' legs, caviar and quail eggs in aspic I have no way of knowing, but the everyday diet from the middle class on down was usually pretty plain. Meat, fish, veggies, soup and pudding were the usual items on the table. Seasonings were salt and pepper.

If my home was typical (and I believe it was) things like garlic were rarities: the only time I remember my parents searching some out was when our Irish Setter, Pat, was sick and the vet recommended the odorous bulb. Similarly, olive oil was a pharmaceutical substance in a drugstore bottle, to be warmed and used as an earache remedy. Mushrooms were a rare treat eaten only by my father. He preferred them fried to a crisp. Spaghetti came out of a can. Cheese was cheddar or perhaps Philadelphia Cream. Avocados? No. Shrimps? Likewise. Fried chicken? Never. Pizza, pepperoni, donairs and quiche didn't appear until decades later.

One thing that acted against fancy fare was the difficulty of preparation before the age of Qwik this and Ezee that. Even

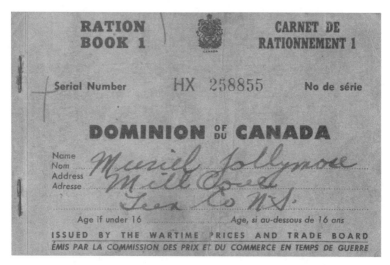

If it was good to eat, it was rationed.

simple treats were difficult enough. Chocolate pudding began with blocks of Baker's solid unsweetened chocolate. A chicken dinner required dragging handfuls of guts out of the bird. Macaroni and cheese needed a grater and some elbow grease. Tapioca came from a box of hard little pellets subjected to a lot of boiling. Junket, which now defines a trip made by an official at public expense, was a white, creamy dessert made of milk and rennet tablets that came out of a small cylindrical box (and I defy you to find any of those on today's supermarket shelves).

Other staples, now largely disappeared, included finnan haddie, the smoked haddock that we were served at least once a week, and lemon snow pudding, a concoction of fresh lemon juice, egg whites and custard. Wonderful!

I was the champion picky eater of peninsular Halifax, I'm sure. Bread I liked — even unbaked bread dough out of the bowl. I was warned this would immediately give me a case of intestinal worms, but that didn't stop me (and I never got worms). Any kind of candy or dessert was fine. Peanut butter, of course. And, for some reason, lima beans. There were some few other comestibles that I allowed to pass my lips, but I was no adventurer. I can still remember my mother's pleading that I "just try" one abomination or another: things like pot roast or meatloaf. Nix.

On the occasional Sunday, our family was invited to the house of a clergyman's widow a few doors up South Street for dinner (now, of course, known as lunch). I dreaded it. After a lengthy grace, the table was laden with things like turbot in white sauce and creamed parsnips. Yak! My mission was simply stated but difficult: a sleight of hand meant to hide as much of the frightful fare away while pretending to munch heartily. If I was successful (and I usually was) I got home undetected, whereupon I was faced with the task of unloading fish, vegetables and unidentified morsels out of my pants pockets and into the garbage. This is not exaggeration. I really did smuggle out whole platefuls of the good widow's masterpieces in this fashion.

All that has changed. At the time of this writing, there is no food (with the possible exception of slimy okra) that I don't like, and it grieves me to think of the delicious treats that went from English bone china into my sticky pockets. I think the later development of a wide-ranging palate began because of peer pressure during visits with my adolescent buddies to ballparks and restaurants. My introduction to hot dogs took place at Ken's Canteen next to the Dingle park across the Northwest Arm. All the other guys were having one. My first hamburger was purchased at the concession on the Wanderer's grounds during a ball game: a patty pressed postage stamp thin by a sturdy spatula. Same incentive: the boys were having one.

Likewise, my first encounter with fish and chips took place one Boy Scout Apple Day, when several of us were assigned a downtown district in which to sell our wares. It was a wretched autumn morning, soggy with driven rain. As the largesse of the residents and passers-by diminished, we retreated to the warmth of a downtown lunch counter. As we shook the water out of our uniforms one of the bunch, a boy named Bobby, said, "Hey! Let's have fish and chips. My treat." Fish. The very word gagged me. But once more peer pressure prevailed, and I said I'd give it a try. After all, I was already adept at pocketing ample portions of seafood. Voila! I was hooked. The deep-fried, battered haddock was delectable.

At the end of the feast, there was only one baffling question. Bobby was no more affluent than the rest of us. How was he going to pay the bill for several stuffed scouts? With insouciance, our buddy reached for the cardboard coin box holding his take for the morning. It was so sodden it was coming apart. Bobby coolly peeled off the lid, counted out enough apple money to pay the cheque, and we departed. I was blushing with the knowledge I had been a party to larceny. But the peer thing kicked in again, and I stayed mum, though half expecting the Police Division of Boy Scouts of Canada to descend on our party at any moment, handcuffs at the ready. Now, when I eat fish and chips, my first bite is sometimes sullied by the guilty memory of the day I first tried it.

When it came to restaurant dining, our city was full of lunch counters, cafés, Chinese eateries and so-called tea rooms. But the only full-scale restaurant I recall was the Green Lantern on Barrington Street, so popular in wartime that there were long queues at the door. The old place, long a Halifax favourite, had been

Fine dining at The Green Lantern.

given a sparkling art deco interior as the thirties arrived, and in my view was the most "modern" place in town. Its cachet was such that it had its own monogrammed crockery to complement the gleaming chrome, leather and marble.

At Babcock's and Russell's, both tea rooms on the north side of Quinpool Road, I learned the delights of a hot chicken sandwich followed by a sundae. One I liked a lot was called a David Harum, available then at most soda fountains. It was a concoction of strawberry, pineapple and other gooey stuff. I wondered for years where the delicacy got its name, and it wasn't until the advent of the Internet that my curiosity impelled me to find out.

David Harum was the titular hero of a bestselling, late nineteenth-century book by Edward Noyes Westcott. Has a ring to it, eh? It was one of those cracker-barrel dialect books popular at the time, the story of a small-town American banker and his homespun philosophies. As popular as it might have been, I have no idea how it lent its name to an ice cream delight (and neither, it seems, does the Internet).

Other names were easier to attribute. The Garden View, owned and operated by the Fong family, was (of course) both on and in view of Spring Garden Road. Cameron's lunch counter at Sackville and Barrington was that family's contribution. Norman's, near the corner of Morris and Hollis, was the enterprise of a man whose all-seeing eyes unceasingly swept the room from the cash desk. This vigilance was, to me, a particular warning against adolescent misbehaviour, given that I often dated his daughter.

The Diana Sweets, just east of Robie on Spring Garden, merits special mention. The Sweets, an Lebanese family (Joe, Tommy and Pop) had once lived on Upper Water Street and sustained the family through stevedoring on the waterfront and pushing peddlers' carts around town. By the dawn of the forties, they had established their iconic hangout for Dalhousie students, athletes and sports fans. The place was never known by the name on its front window. Rather, it was just "Joe's."

By the time I entered adulthood, the city was slowly changing to the wonderful dining mosaic it is now. The French Casino on Gottingen Street, run by Jean LaLonde, was a big step. I still remember their *Tournedos Rossini*: butter-fried tenderloin chunks served on a crouton with a nice little slab of foie gras. It took a while for some of us to stop referring to the dish as tornados, but sophistication arrived.

Italian food followed, with Joe Pillateri presenting the first pizza to hit Halifax in the neighbourhood where Scotia Square stands today. Hoagie brought an American-style steak house to

Quinpool Road. Gradually, we came to enjoy restaurant foods from around the world, each a boost to our dining discernment. Turkish, Russian, Japanese, Thai, Korean and dozens more international delicacies became part of the scene, and our yellow pages displayed choices that, once upon a time, would have found their way into my pockets. Now, there's never even a smudge left on any plate that's put before me. And my ever-expanding waistline carries the proof that I've become a well-practiced gourmand.

6

Down the Bank

THE NEIGHBOURHOOD IN WHICH I was lucky enough to grow up was essentially suburban during the thirties. I have an early photograph of Dalhousie Street, taken by my father before it was built-up. It shows the street from South Street down to Oakland Road (both gravel roads at the time). There's a birch tree almost halfway down and a bare field stretching behind the whole block. Although our house faced Dalhousie Street, it was numbered on the back door as 392 South at the time, probably as an easier address to locate than one on a new and little-known street.

The street was actually built on a shelf-like fill of subsoil and rock, which created a steep bank on its west side. South Street was built on, and formed the base of, an approximate isosceles triangle with the uninhabited sides formed by South Connaught (now Beaufort) and Dalhousie. That triangle of tangled undergrowth was infested with clothes-grabbing burdocks ("buzzies" we called them) and beggar's ticks. There were a couple of bedrock outcroppings, anthills and, behind an old house on the north side, a small garbage dump. That undeveloped section was known to us as Down the Bank. It was an autonomous, sovereign

The centre of my world — Dalhousie, my home and down the bank.

territory and we kids deemed ourselves its legitimate freeholders.

It was criss-crossed with paths, kept bare by our single-file sa-
faris. A large, easily climbed birch at its centre was our citadel,
with seating enough for all. That tree could become a lofty ship,
a military redoubt, a lookout tower or any other expedient venue
our minds could conjure up. Being younger than the rest of the
Down the Bank denizens, I was consequently the lowest ranked
of all, often singled out as the butt of pranks and an object of mild
ridicule. Low-end bullying, I suppose, and, essentially, the price of
belonging. The leader was a young adventurer called Donald, who
lived just down the street from me. He was brave, imaginative,
charismatic, smart and assertive. He was also rash, untruthful and
resistant to authority. His supremacy went unquestioned, especially by me, as I experienced an early introduction to peer pressure.

One of Donald's oft-repeated and direst warnings concerned
the "Shipley Gang," reputedly made up of older youths from the

43

fearsome North End of Halifax. He cautioned us all repeatedly that if the gang were to appear in our territory, we were goners unless we followed his orders without question. He had a vast reserve of Shipley stories. They carried knives and bombs. They kidnapped other kids and dragged them to the North End, where they were forced to eat boiling hot porridge. They peed on people. They stole, pillaged and plundered. And they hated South Enders.

One of Donald's anti-Shipley precautions was the digging of several foot-deep pits in the network of Down the Bank paths. These we covered with sticks, tufts of grass and leaves until they were undetectable. Only we knew where they were. I doubt that these "mantraps," as Donald called them, would have inflicted anything more than a twisted ankle, but Donald assured us that they were helping him keep our preserve safe from intruders.

The time came when he confirmed his role as defence minister, even if the threat to our safety was a product of his own overactive imagination. We were up the tree on a fine spring afternoon. From below we heard the sound of footsteps and voices. We looked down to see three boys, bigger than Donald himself, looking up at us. Not the Shipleys, perhaps, but in our protector's eyes, an implicit threat — though one that remained implicit. There was no challenge, no taunting, no truculence from them. They just looked. But their presence was enough for Donald. "Stay in the tree," he shouted.

Then, with a dramatic flair worthy of Errol Flynn, he hurled himself out of his branch (which was some fourteen feet from the ground) and landed directly on top of them. Bodies flew everywhere. There was yelling and confusion. From its midst came Donald's shout: "Run for your lives!" I was the first to take that command instantly and fully to heart, sliding down the tree trunk, scrambling up the bank and running home as though pursued by all the imps of hottest hell. It was days before I went Down the Bank again. When I did, there was no explanation, no clarification from Donald. And I, as a lowly apprentice, was not about to press him for details. I knew my place.

It was not long after that incident that Donald's family prepared to move from the neighbourhood, forcing his abdication. But he had one daring exploit yet to perform. It involved a family living on the South Street edge of Down the Bank. They were quiet, pleasant people, but Donald had taken umbrage at some (probably fabricated) slight and was running a one-sided feud. He had told his disciples more than once of the act of vengeance he'd planned. The family's garage was built on concrete piers, and extended over a sharp drop in their backyard. The space below the garage was enclosed with interlaced brown wooden laths. Donald's plan was to sneak out of his bedroom in the dead of night, steal up the street, and smash those laths into matchwood.

That was too much for me to get my seven-year-old head around. South End boys didn't do things like that, not actual criminal acts! This had to be Donald's powerful imagination at its most intense. Then came the morning I looked out the window and saw that his plot had materialized. There was the garage in question with every one of the carefully installed laths shattered into splinters. And they still lay like that the following week when Donald's family left the neighbourhood. I have a feeling that their departure was a good thing, at least for me.

However, if it was the end of Donald's dictatorship, it didn't end my dread of the Shipley gang. Even as an adult, when I started collecting Halifax city directories, I checked the listings for Shipleys.

Nothing much. Only one or two families, and none of them in the North End. Then, while searching the Internet for something unrelated, what did I come across? The story of a noted band of brigands who terrorized part of Yorkshire in the early nineteenth century. They went by the name of the village that was their head-quarters: the Shipley Gang. The inventive Donald had read of them as a boy, and had used his research to recreate the story to his own specifications in 1930s Halifax. Evidently he subscribed to the ad-age, "Never let the truth get in the way of a good story."

The dictator's departure didn't end activity Down the Bank, but he took most of the hazards with him. One peaceful episode I remember from post-Donald days is the time some older kids, including one called Gibby, decided to have a cookout in a little spot perhaps too near the dump, but still convenient. Somewhat condescendingly, I was invited to attend. My instructions were to bring a potato and a spoon from home, which I dutifully did.

When three or four of us had gathered at the appointed spot, potatoes in hand, Gibby lit a fire of twigs and small sticks. We hunkered there for what seemed a very long time, feeding the fire and then letting it burn down to embers. With reverence, each potato was buried in the glowing heap and we resumed hunker-ing. At this point, Gibby produced several rashers of bacon, and distributed one to each of us. His instruction were to wrap the bacon around a green stick (plenty of those at hand) and toast it over the coals like a marshmallow. My heart sank. Potatoes were among the three or four substances I consented to eat at home, but bacon was not. Still, I knew I could rely on the food-conceal-ing skills I'd developed over time.

But by now, the potatoes were ready to be dug out. One by one, smoking, coal-black lumps were exhumed from their pyre and set on the ground. . .one each. Surely this was a joke! The things were burnt beyond redemption. Only when Gibby produced a jackknife and sliced the first one open did I realize what a treasure lay before us. The contrast between the black char of the jacket and the mealy, gleaming, pure white inside was incredible. It looked like a royal feast — and so it was. I guided each steaming spoonful into my mouth until I was left with the burnt, crisp skin. And I ate that too.

The bacon came next. Partly goaded by watchful eyes, and partly emboldened by the success with the potato, I gingerly bit off a crunchy corner, poised to spit quickly if necessary. It wasn't. The salty, crunchy morsel was better than anything I'd ever tasted till then, and as good as I ever ate afterwards. Gibby nodded in approval as I wolfed it down. Though it might have been only a potato and a piece of bacon to the others, to me it was a rite of passage. I'd cooked and eaten like a Big Guy, Down the Bank. I had arrived.

Of course, the time eventually came when that overgrown triangular tract was built on and Down the Bank was lost to us. The first house on the west side was a cozy cottage built by a Mr. Todd and his sister. I was pushing adolescence by then. I watched as the dynamite holes were drilled into our best bedrock ledge, one that had served us well as a British submarine. Damped by bundles of alder poles and announced by a wheezy tin horn, the subsequent blasts created a hole for a cellar as the end of Down the Bank got under way. It was the death of a nation.

7

All for Free

IN THE THIRTIES, THE STUDLEY campus of Dalhousie had but a few buildings, with the dignified architecture of Andrew Cobb predominating. These included the (then) Arts and Science Buildings; the original Public Archives of Nova Scotia; Shirreff Hall; the new gymnasium built to replace one mysteriously burned to the ground in May, 1931 (about three months before I was born) and the so-called Murray Homestead, an old residence dating from the days when the Studley grounds were a private estate. There was also an old coach house or garden house topped by a cupola that served as a storage building for the groundskeepers. And that was all.

The northwest corner of the old grounds was occupied by King's College, with its own quad partly surrounded by residences, the main building, the chapel and the President's lodge, all of them connected both above and below ground. The whole complex, Dalhousie and King's, was bounded to the north, the south and part of the west by the fine old drystone wall that had surrounded the estate, much of which remains today. The east side of the campus was bordered by the houses of LeMarchant Street, and there was a short row of homes along Coburg Road where

Naval training at His Majesty's Canadian "Ship" King's 1941–1945.

the Howe Hall residence now stands. A special half acre right across from our home was occupied by the Studley Quoit Club.

Near the club grounds there was a small woods that ran east from the Oxford Street side, a place of birdsongs and shadows. The athletic grounds now known as Wickwire Field was the combat zone of the Dalhousie Tigers, who played rugby to the strains of a hearty song from the bleachers: "Come sons of old Dalhousie, cheer your lusty team! Stand up and holler for your men of steel and steam."

We boys found plenty of space, much variety and many opportunities for adventure at Studley. A couple of gravelled roadways were flanked by trees, and a small brook ran east-west near the Archives. One of our number created a novel portmanteau word combining "brook" and "drink," and our name for the tiny waterway was the Brink.

The stone foundation of the burned gymnasium was covered by tar and gravelled roofing, not a thing of any beauty. But it provided one of the best adventures, because there was a tunnel that ran underground from its bowels to the basement of the new gym, which we were able to access (though I forget just how). Negotiating that chamber in the bedrock was like something out of the *Boy's Own Annual* and, thankfully, we were never discovered within it. A similar exploit was offered at King's, where there was a tunnel full of fat steam pipes beneath the buildings that we were able to get into (again, I forget how). But the best exploit was to be found in the main King's building, where there was a great room served by a dumb waiter, a very small elevator operated by ropes and pulleys, presumably used to carry banquet meals from the basement kitchen to the big hall and a second-storey room above it. We'd take turns scrunching into the thing to be given a jerky trip up and down the dark shaft. Again, we were never discovered in the operation of this indoor amusement ride. Obviously, campus security was not what it became in later years. I would entreat young readers to recognize that my youth was spent in a more trusting and less restricted era when adventure had to be found outdoors and for free, and that computer games would have been exciting enough for us boys if only they'd existed. As it was, everything outside the front door of home was there to be explored, accessed and enjoyed.

Another of these adventure grounds was the "horse field," adjoining the railway track between Jubilee Road and Geldert Street, now upgraded to a park. The big sign at the entrance states that the area was once pluralized as the "horse fields," which it never was to my memory. Wasn't much to it but scrubby vegetation and footpaths.

The Morris Street boulevard between Robie and South Park, now part of University Avenue, was a handy place to meet friends under the pines (which, incidentally, produced the biggest, most handsome cones in town). The place sticks in my mind as the spot where I was first exposed to Kipling's "The Young British Soldier," recited at length by one of the Fry brothers, Rupert or Bill, both of whom were a bit older and too cool for words. It was then I realized, with delight, that one could enjoy verse and be cool as well. . .not that I ever became remotely so.

Franklyn Park, now the site of Chain Rock Drive and other upscale streets, was an open swath with a dance pavilion at its centre and the tumbled old penitentiary at its edge. We didn't resort to it much, because it bordered the far more interesting Point Pleasant Park.

Point Pleasant, with its forts, batteries and bridle paths was, to us, a miraculous playground. By war's end, the World War II emplacements had been vacated, and we got to forage for the left behind carbon arc rods of the massive searchlights that had probed the sky during air raid exercises. There wasn't much to them. They were just black pointed cylinders, but we prized them as "real army stuff" until the novelty wore off and they joined the cinders in the family ashcan.

The older fortifications, with their parapets and casemates, evoked Kipling's British soldiery as well as the Fry brothers did. The Martello Tower, in those days, was accessible to inventive boys, if not the public, and we marvelled at the gloomy and seemingly impregnable space inside the eight-foot-thick masonry walls. Of particular interest were the metal chutes in the flooring of the projecting gun platforms. We convinced ourselves they were meant to disgorge quantities of boiling oil or molten lead on any enemy that got close enough. In rational retrospect, they were probably there to carry off rainwater. Near the tower entrance lay another attraction, the great, glacier-grooved patch of bedrock, where we'd trace the striations with a fingertip and try to imagine what the world was like when they were made.

Grafton Park, where the Halifax Memorial Library stood, was one of the few shady spots to be found downtown where a lad could find a bit of turf on which to sit and observe the passing parade. That was also where, during the VE Day riot of 1945, we goggle-eyed lads were stunned by the sight of a bacchanal beyond our wildest imaginings. And, as I later learned, hundreds of poverty-stricken Haligonians of long-past generations lay beneath the sod of the little patch, placed there when it was the burial place of the town's paupers.

Gorsebrook Golf Course, the remains of the expansive Enos Collins estate, was a poorly managed organization by the time my pals and I were old enough to swing a club. It must have been, because we played endless rounds using scavenged balls, scrounged wooden-shafted clubs and broken tees with never a marshal to bid us be gone. We must have been the last generation to use the terms "mashie," "spoon," "niblick" and "midiron" for the sorry sticks in our possession. But we were aware enough of golf's galaxy to adopt, while playing, such names as Sam Snead, Byron Nelson and Bobby Jones. Most of the remaining holes of the original eighteen were north of Inglis Street, with a couple more (eleven and twelve, as I remember) to the south, where Saint Mary's University now stands. The clubhouse, the door of which we never darkened, was the Collins mansion just off Tower Road. It had a long, decaying shed attached which had been the Collins stables in the reign of the carriage horse.

But to end where this began, back on the Studley campus, I must mention a small plot of that acreage that was home to the Studley Quoit Club. It was a fenced-off quad with three sets of quoit beds: sod-sided patches of raked earth, somewhat like a horseshoe bed, but slanted. The quoits themselves were circles of brass or bronze, tossed toward the whitewashed wooden stake at the centre of each bed. Every weekday it was a place for our gang of kids to play games or just hang out on the spectator benches on the sides. But, come Saturday morning, there was a transformation. The only paid staff of the club was a cockney gentleman named Jim who arrived in the neighbourhood early in the day and re-paired to the Burns property, three doors up South Street from the corner of Dalhousie. The Burnses lived in a handsome, gin-gerbread-trimmed house with a big, square barn behind it where the paraphernalia of the club was stored. There was a sizeable tent, groundskeeping tools, a bucket of whitewash, the heavy set of quoits, a blackboard, flags, a folding table and, most peculiar of all, an old-fashioned telephone of the wooden box type.

All of this Jim laboriously wheeled across the street, load by load, in a wheelbarrow and deployed in its proper place (nearly always trailed by us young observers). With the beds raked and the stakes whitewashed, the tent erected and the table set up, there remained two jobs for Jim. One was to hang the telephone on a tall pine near the tent and connect to it the bare ends of two insulated wires. The other was to run the White Ensign of the Royal Navy up the flagpole, a meaningful moment in that Studley was the only land-based club to possess the right to do so, an honour bestowed by a former admiral posted in Halifax. Some of the kids, myself included, learned this tidbit early, along with the information that the club had been visited by British royalty including Edward VII and his grandson Edward Prince of Wales (the latter in 1919 at the height of his popularity).

By the time everything was in place, Jim shooed his "audience" away before the first members arrived. I don't remember him setting out any liquor, so maybe a designated member brought in the ardent spirits that were served during the afternoon. Apparently the club was famous for its well-guarded recipe for Squadron Punch, and even as a child its potency was obvious to me as I watched some of the members giddily reeling down South Street at the end of the afternoon. I asked my mother about this tendency, and she attributed it to "a touch of the sun." I knew better.

The time came, in 1939, when my own chance to see British royalty leave footprints on the quoit club turf was promised but, alas, it was not to be. The original plan for the famous Royal Visit of George VI and Queen Elizabeth included a stop-off at Studley, and a granite-block stile was built into the South Street wall to make their access easier. Plans changed, and the walk around the grounds was cancelled, though the glittering couple did drive down South Street, right past our house, in their open limousine. I was perched on our steps with a glass of water just in case the beautiful queen was thirsty and ordered the driver to stop. The royal request for my cold water never came to pass.

Eventually, the quoit club disbanded and the Burns home and barn were razed for the Dalplex development, but the granite blocks of the stile are still there, incorporated into the south wall of the Studley estate. And two of the most beloved members of British royalty drove within a few yards of it.

In my youth, freshwater ponds were more plentiful in Halifax, and boys found them good adventure spots. There was one in Marlborough Woods (inevitably called "Marble Woods" in our lexicon). It lay south of Inglis Street and west of the Collins lands now occupied by Saint Mary's University. Although early maps describe it as Ritchie's Pond, we called it Frog Pond, and indeed it was a good spot to watch the evolution of frogs from eggs to tadpoles to nimble green swimmers. Too shallow to pose a serious risk of drowning, it was deep enough to send an incautious youngster sloshing home with his lumberman's rubbers full of reeking, muddy water. The surrounding tall pines and tangled undergrowth gave the impression that the civilized world, with its restrictions, had been left safely behind.

During wartime, the occasional serviceman and his sweetie would resort to the area in search of the same sort of privacy we boys found there. Surprised by a command to "Get the hell out of here!" issued by the male partner of a couple snuggled beneath a blue or khaki greatcoat, we'd run (snickering all the way) back to the staid and civil streets to the north.

Eventually, those streets intruded into the balsam-scented sanctuary of Marlborough Woods. Robie Street, Marlborough, Bellevue and Greenwood Avenues extended south across Inglis Street, and Ritchie Drive was created parallel to them. I've often wondered just which of today's houses were built over that froggy habitat, and how persistently the pungent pond water might have dampened their basements over time.

On South Street, just east of the Dickensian brick façade of the City Home (called the Poor House by most) riffled the waters of the Pogie. This pond, the derivation of whose name I've never discovered, was eventually covered by the IWK complex. In any event, we found it too forbidding for recreation. There were those who occasionally skated during winter cold spells, but in one section the ice was weakened by a steam pipe that emerged from the north bank. Probably part of some system within the nearby Victoria General Hospital or the City Home itself, this vaporous hazard kept me and my mates from daring even a trial skim of the treacherous surface.

Another, more public, lagoon was the Egg Pond, which graced the North Common just east of Bell Road. Originally fed from a long-filled swamp near the intersection of Chebucto Road and Windsor Street, the aptly named oval tarn was edged by a masonry wall. Lucky was the lad who could sail his model sailboat across from shore to shore without having to wade out to retrieve it. Now, of course, the Egg Pond, too, has disappeared, and has given way to a newer pastime: skateboarding and bicycle stunting.

From the Egg Pond, the waters of Freshwater Brook were piped underground, running southeast. On its way through the Public Gardens the brook resurfaced to form the Duck Pond and a short stretch of brook, before descending beneath South Park

Street as far as Fenwick, where it gurgled its subterranean way to the harbour.

Steele's Pond once graced the Greenbank Road, leading along the harbour shoreline to Point Pleasant Park near the foot of Point Pleasant Drive. By my day, the fashionable Greenbank Road, once the site of stately mansions, had given way to the rail yards and piers of the Ocean Terminals, and had become a rutted dirt roadway that edged the near-original outline of the pond. Too far from home to provide much attraction to us as preteens, in time it afforded a secluded spot for a young couple to park a parent's reluctantly lent car after a dance or a movie. The pastime of necking, more moderate than what we hear constitutes today's teenage romantic adventures, was referred to (with a knowing wink) as "watching the submarine races."

Then there was Quarry Pond, up the hill from Steele's and just inside the so-called Golden Gates of Point Pleasant. This jagged punchbowl, left after building stone had been excavated from the bedrock, was said to be bottomless. We boys had to check out this rumour with a length of fishing line and a sinker (and I must admit to our disappointment at dispelling it). But unlike many the venues of old, Quarry Pond today looks precisely as it did to youths of my generation.

There were, indeed, other open spaces available to me and my contemporaries, but these were our favourites. Schoolyards were uninviting, graveyards were spooky, Flynn Park was too far away, the Halifax Commons was bare and gritty. No complaints, though. We got through our early years with plenty of choices. The Great Outdoors was all ours. No dues, no membership requirements, no green fees.

How lucky we were.

8

Rambles

DURING THE FIRST TEN YEARS of my life, excursions outside my South End neighbourhood were few, and therefore memorable. The first I can recall is being taken on a walk by my young and very beautiful mother. We walked and walked, all the way from Dalhousie Street to the foot of what was called Inglis Street Extension, then a newly created road. Near the Winwick railway bridge, there was a small bit of pasture, and, tethered in its middle, a cow.

What happened next has stayed with me, principally because my mother never let me forget it. In fact, over the years she regaled many a friend with the tale of how I bravely ventured nearer and nearer the grazing bovine while she sternly called me back. I paid no attention, and she called again. I toddled on, getting quite near the creature. Again she called. Again I ignored her. Then, all of a sudden, the cow swung her head around, fixed me with a baleful stare, and trumpeted a thunderous moo. At that, as the parental tale had it, I ran back to safety as fast as my legs would take me, all the while obediently shrilling, "I'se coming, Mummy, I'se coming!" When driving past the 900 block of

Beaufort these days do I still get a shiver of cowphobia? No, but I do look at the tidy row of houses on the east side of the street and think back to when a modest collection of cow flops and their manufacturer occupied the space.

My first real foray into "the country" began when I was still a pretty small kid. That was when I went on a family skating expedition to Frog Pond, beside the Purcell's Cove Road. I was small enough to be wearing leggings and using those useless, four bladed clunkers called sleigh skates. Any kid who could scuff across a waxed floor in stockings could do something similar on ice as a sleigh skater. Though my recollection of the trip to Frog Pond is generally hazy, one moment is crystallized in my brain cells. I pushed off from the edge of the pond, skated (or rather, shuffled) my way out onto the ice, and quite promptly went through it. In that instant, I had learned what pop psychologists now refer to as a life lesson: don't skate too close to rocks, because the ice tends to be thinner there. No real harm was done, because I only went in to the top of my leggings. I don't think I ever tried those stupid, quadruple-bladed contraptions again.

After that, our skating trips were mostly to Chocolate Lake, where there stood a long, wooden rack operated as a concession. You paid a nickel, and were allotted a hook on which to hang your street shoes. Our family trick was to put hot baked potatoes into the skates on leaving home, which kept them warm on the way to the lake. When we changed, the potatoes went into the shoes, maintaining at least a slight warmth in them until we were ready for the walk home. By then I had a proper pair of what were called "tube" skates. But I still performed on them as if scuffing across a hardwood floor.

My first expedition beyond the city limits without my parents

Rookie in the horsebun hockey league.

was a truly liberating occasion. The occasion was that then-common, now-rare phenomenon: a Sunday School picnic. Our troop of pious (well, at least not evil) little travellers gathered on the steps of King's College, where Sunday School for young Anglicans was then held. Everybody carried a bag lunch of sandwiches. I can't imagine I was shod with anything other than my prized Sisman Scampers.

Scampers were fairly new on the market at the time, and were considered pretty special. In fact, they were a gotta-have-it brand like the top-end sneakers of today, though in construction they were leather jobs more resembling a Hush Puppy style. They had, as I recall, cork insoles that provided a comfortable walk. The distinguishing mark, equivalent of today's Nike "Swoosh" logo, was a big cursive "S" that looked more like a treble clef, stitched into the side of the shoe.

With a couple of valiant Sunday School teachers as our safari guides and disciplinarians, we made our way to the foot of Oakland Road and down the steps to Boutilier's Ferry landing, chattering all the way about the exploits that lay before us. There were few enough of us that one boatload got all of us across. Then the trudge began, up the steep dirt road, past the little stone church, through the rustic village of Jollimore, across the Purcell's Cove Road and into what the *Boy's Own Annual* readers among us might have thought of as The Interior.

Soft pine needles alternated with crunchy gravel underfoot as we left the Williams Lake Road and trod along a narrow path to the edge of that beautiful body of water, without a single building on its shore. As a city boy in a family with no car, such near-wilderness was new to me. Sunday School kids no longer, we were one with comic page heroes Tim and Spud of the Ivory Patrol, on the track of dastardly smugglers on a jungle path. We slogged on, told by our adult guides that another, more remote destination lay ahead: Colpitt Lake. Two in one day! When we got to quiet little Colpitt, only the rustle of leaves and the unwrapping of our wax-papered lunch packages met our ears. No traffic sounds, no train whistles. We had followed the call of the wild, and found it enthralling.

Me at St. Moritz aka South Street.

The same general area provided two more forays before the 1930s came to an end. One was a Boy Scout hike to the Rocking Stone, during which we had to perform the traditional scout fire-lighting contest: one match, no paper, with the prize going to the boy who could bring his billy-can of water to a boil first. We also got to rock the Stone, which by then needed a long spruce pole as a lever. In earlier days, before a bunch of garrison soldiers overdid the shoving and spoiled the rock's perfect balance, the trick could have been done unaided by the scrawny members of the Beaver Patrol of the 9th Halifax Troop. Once again, this trip seemed well into the deep interior of Halifax County. Now the Rocking Stone lends it name to a paved suburban road, and the sophisticated youngsters of the computer game set would probably yawn with disdain at the prospect. "What? Just rocking a boulder? Get real!"

And just off the east side of the Purcell's Cove Road, near the Pond Playhouse, lies the first (well, only) mountain I ever climbed. My father took me there to scale the heights once or twice. It's not much more than a big lump of bedrock, but Mount Misery has a better ring to it than Lump Misery. In later years I took my own son up the Mount and found it much the same: a pudding-shaped protuberance covered with glacial striations. The difference from my own first visit was that we drove there over pavement all the way, the rock was littered with broken beer bottles, the rush of traffic eclipsed the rustle of leaves, and the Mount was surrounded by a neighbourhood of modern homes.

The tiny, stone St. Augustine's church of my youth has been succeeded by a more modern wooden edifice on Purcell's Cove Road. Nobody fishes commercially out of Jollimore these days. One can't rent a rowboat or canoe as once one could. No make-and-break ferry. But, thank heavens, the stately Memorial Tower still reigns over Jollimore.

9

Grade School

MY SCHOOL DAYS BEGAN AT the privately run Sea Gates West End Junior School, which occupied the bottom flat of a large house on the South side of Quinpool Road just west of Bloomingdale. My two years there covered the equivalent of kindergarten and grade one in the public schools. What faint memories I have of the place involve smocks, finger paints, crayons, marbles and very small chairs at low tables.

Then came the big time, the transfer to grade two at Le-Marchant Street School under the tutelage of Mrs. MacKenzie. LeMarchant consisted of two buildings. The brick bungalow or "Little School" housed kindergarten to grade three. The older, wooden building to the south, called the "Big School," was occupied by grades four to nine.

The Bungalow was relatively new and airy and, once I got used to the protocols, safe enough. The biggest and earliest mistake I made about schoolyard behaviour was due to the fact that, as a pre-schooler, I'd spent many happy hours perched on my grandparents' steps at 36 Walnut Street, directly across from the schoolyard, watching the kids at play. From observation I knew

Me, in the obligatory outfit of leather cap, wool britches and tall boots.

that many school kids derived enjoyment from jumping on one another's backs. So, when the recess bell rang on my first day at LeMarchant, I filed out to the schoolyard and jumped on the back of a kid I selected at random. Unfortunately, he was not only a sizeable lad, but one not well disposed to back-jumping. I've not forgotten his reaction. First, he yelled at me, using a phrase now disappeared from schoolyards: "Hang off!" Then he threw me violently to the hard-packed, gravelly ground and left me, my head spinning, wondering what part of the procedure had gone wrong.

My year with the kindly Mrs. MacKenzie over, I proceeded the next fall to Miss Mitchell's grade three. Miss Mitchell was old, and had decades of stern disciplinary experience behind her. There was no fun in that class, except when the singing of the morning hymns took place. Yes, though there were always Jewish kids in our classes, we all sang Christian hymns every morning. "Tell me the Stories of Jesus," "Mothers of Salem," "Jesus Bids me Shine" and others were tuneful favourites and enjoyable to sing, but the real enjoyment came from observing our leader. Miss Mitchell not only had a treble voice, but a loosely hanging, crepe-fleshed triple chin that shuddered and quivered in wonderful waggles as she sang. Her pulsating vibrato never stayed on pitch for more than a moment before rippling past the note, upwards and downwards, exactly like the reverberations of a musical saw.

Moving up to the Big School made for a change, especially of surroundings. The large, ancient building was dusty, dingy and Dickensian, with a pervasive miasma of chalk dust and damp. What my first year in the place lacked in decent surroundings was more than made up for by our grade four teacher, dear Miss Lucas. She was quiet, kind and younger than most of the other teachers. And, unlike some of her colleagues, she obviously loved children.

It is therefore somewhat ironic that I got my first strapping from this sweet soul. I'm quite certain the punishment was richly deserved, although I've long forgotten the offence. What is perfectly clear in my memory, though, is waiting for my licking in the cloakroom where it was to be carried out. As a neophyte I didn't know quite what to expect, but fervently hoped it wouldn't

British evacuee children arrive at Pier 21 — friends for "the duration."

be severe enough to make me cry. In came Miss Lucas, wide rubber strap in hand and gave me a quiet lecture on what kind of behaviour was not to be tolerated. I obediently held out my right hand and the strap swung down and met my palm. The sting was slight, and I knew immediately that I wouldn't be brought to tears. But I could never have predicted what was to happen as the succeeding smacks came down. I stood there dry-eyed but, to my amazed embarrassment, it was poor Miss Lucas who erupted into a flurry of hot tears. Needless to say those tears, not the strap, meant I never committed another corporal offence in her class.

Miss Naylor in grade five was substantially different — a woman lacking kindness, good humour and any empathy for kids other than her favourites. At least once, her malevolence reached sadistic proportions, prompting a scene that has stayed with me since. My friend Bobby Goss ("Gupper" to his buddies) was the unfortunate victim. Gupper was a bit of a rebel, a little on the wild side, but a good, steady companion.

One afternoon, after Miss Naylor called the class to order, she noted that we'd been given our quarter's artwork envelopes to take home before the morning session let out. Then she told us that somebody had torn up his envelope and its contents and strewn the scraps all over the schoolyard. Warming to her task, she went on to relate that the School Inspector had visited LeMarchant over the noontime, and had been appalled at this disgraceful scene. Then, with barely suppressed delight, she said that the great man had picked up one of the scraps and had read the name of the culprit in the margin. Pausing for effect, she slowly raised her arm and pointed a finger at the hapless Gupper, saying, "And that boy's name is Robert Goss," in much the same way as one imagines Emile Zola might have intoned "J'accuse" at the time of the Drefus trial. A shudder of awed anticipation ran through her audience as she continued, "And, Robert Goss, you are going to be strapped." All eyes were on Gupper, as he started to rise from his seat with a plucky but fragile smirk on his face. The teacher stopped him. "Not yet, Robert," she intoned. "Sit in your seat and think about it, and you'll get your punishment before dismissal."

That did it for poor Gupper, who sat weeping and red-eyed for the rest of the session and eventually got his whacks in the coat-room, within full earshot of the class. He bore that better than he had the psychological torment that preceded it, was surrounded by well-wishers in the schoolyard afterward and went home a hero.

That was the best and worst of the teacher roster at Le-Marchant. Miss Dockrill (grade six) is mostly remembered for reminding us several times an hour that, "Speech is silver, silence is gold," but was otherwise a reasonable teacher. Miss Mitchell (grade seven) was a fine figure of a woman, thanks to corsets that must have been made of triple-layered whalebone and galvanized fence wire. Stern, but fair. Miss Bruce (grade eight) was an enemy: so much so that after one quite unjust strapping from her I colluded with my buddy "Ducker" Ross to burn her in effigy on our driveway after school. She made a fine blaze.

Then it was grade nine taught by the redoubtable Col. C.V. Harris, who had lately been mustered out of the army and returned to teaching. "C.V." brooked no nonsense, but was easily induced to spend a whole period telling yarns instead of cramming our heads with useful learning. His position as principal necessitated his occasional absence from class, and it was during one of these departures that I took the opportunity to loft a large art-gum eraser at the back of Ed Kinley's head. Ed's desk was near the door. Just as the rubber lump left my hand, the door opened and the principal strode in. My trajectory went amiss and, of course, the eraser hit C.V. in the dead centre of his broad forehead. I must have been pretty obvious as the perpetrator, for after blinking hard for a moment, the principal's immediate words were, "All right, Bennet. . .out in the hall!" Mr. Harris was not a coatroom man. Out I went. Out he strode, strap in hand. Five on each hand, hard enough to make me bite my lip. But that was all. Back in the door and class resumed without a hitch. No sadism or psychological agony. All business, and over in under a minute. And that was the end of my corporal punishment experience, during which, like most of my friends, I'd been licked at least once in every grade.

There were bullies at LeMarchant, but I managed immunity through the oldest gambit known to bully bait: I became class clown. It worked, too — why harm the owl that's providing the best hoots? Outside school, it was a different matter. I was always on the lookout for "tough guys" — running, hiding or crossing the street when necessary. But one afternoon, on my way home across the Dalhousie campus, I was caught out; I noticed three bigger guys closing in on me. Nowhere to hide, no street to cross. My heart raced as I realized I was in trouble.

"Are you a Catholic?" asked the biggest of the three. They had to be kids from St. Thomas Aquinas school, and if I admitted to Anglicanism, I was in for a drubbing. I cleared my throat and my mind raced for an answer. For a moment, I considered quoting the Apostle's Creed we intoned every Sunday — the part that said, "I believe in the Holy Catholic Church." I almost blurted out the phrase when I saw an even bigger guy than my tormentors walking down the field.

I knew him at sight. He was a school hockey star named Mac-Neil, already quite famous in Halifax. He lived nearby, on Coburg Road, and he, too, was Catholic. Horrors!

He stopped and sized up the situation, asking what was going on. Nobody said anything. He looked me square in the face and asked, "These guys bothering you?" I looked at the ground and nodded. There was a momentary pause during which my fate seemingly hung in the balance. Then the big fellow spoke. His words were among the sweetest I'd ever heard.

"Leave him alone," he barked. "Get on out of here!"

The bully boys walked away, mumbling something about meaning no harm. They knew better, as did I, but you didn't argue with a hockey hero. My rescuer gave me a reassuring smile and said, "Off you go home."

It didn't take me long. I raced home at full tilt in astonishingly little time, my schoolbag bumping wildly on my backside.

I never forgot that big athlete who saved me from a thumping. He was Dugger McNeil, who went on to glory as one of the top local hockey players of his day, eventually finding a place in the Nova Scotia Sports Hall of Fame.

He also made a career in the field of men's clothing. The top-end store he founded still flourishes on Spring Garden Road, where his name welcomes shoppers on a sign emblazoned "Dugger's."

Such school spirit as existed was boosted infrequently by both a school song and a yell. The song, to the tune of "The British Grenadiers," went:

Some talk of Alexandra and some of Morris Street;

> *Of Richmond, Sir Charles Tupper and such great schools as these.*
> *But of all the schools in Halifax, be they great or small,*
> *We'll try to make LeMarchant the best school of them all!*
> *The school yell, which I only remember yelling in assembly hall, was:*
> *Strawberry shortcake, huckleberry pie;*
> *V-I-C-T-O-R-Y!*
> *Are we in it? Well I guess;*
> *LeMarchant, LeMarchant, yes, yes yes!*

Another aspect of life in the Big School was patriotism, which was brought out strongly by the outbreak of World War II. We bought War Saving Stamps for a quarter apiece and pasted them in a small book for redemption after the war. We collected for the

On His Majesty's Service with the ARP.

Queen's Canadian Fund. Each morning we recited, "I pledge allegiance to the flag and to the Empire for which it stands." Hearts swelling, we sang, "We'll never let the old flag fall, for we love it the best of all" and "The Maple Leaf Forever." We joined cadets, in which I inexplicably ranked as a lieutenant. We turned out for scrap drives and war bond rallies. Some, myself included, joined the ARP (Air Raid Precautions) corps and carried buckets and stirrup pumps in drills. There was even one boy, who'd been kept back a couple of years and was big for his age, who quit school and joined the merchant navy.

Health measures during those years consisted of tuberculin skin tests ("Schick" tests) for susceptibility to diphtheria, inspections for head lice and physical training at wide intervals in the

Here we come a-carolling:(l-r) Jack Dawson, Rick Dawson, Joan Allen, Jane Bennet, Caroline Bennet, Cam Allen and top-hatted yours truly.

schoolyard. Health was also taught as a class, during which we were admonished to drink at least seven full glasses of water a day and towel ourselves vigorously after a bath. Nothing much more.

I always thought that the visiting school nurse should have taken a look at the school basement where the lavatories were. No amount of high-pressure hosing could have erased the filth of that grimy retreat. It was a rock-walled crater festooned with peeling coats of dirty gray whitewash and smutty spiderwebs. The plumbing was ancient and rust stained. And on one wall of the facility there hung a framed and faded motto under cracked, flyspecked glass. It read: Cleanliness is Next to Godliness.

10

Door to Door

THROUGHOUT THE 1930S AND INTO the early 1940s, many commodities were delivered daily to Halifax households. Perhaps the most astonishing service, in the eyes of today's consumer, was provided by the postman. He (and the job was indeed exclusively male back then) provided not one, but two deliveries every weekday, and one on Saturday morning. When insufficient postage was affixed to a parcel or envelope, the doorbell would ring and the neatly uniformed carrier would ask for the amount due before handing over the goods.

While the mail was delivered on foot, there were several commodities that came either daily or sporadically by horse and wagon. Milk, for instance, was heralded by the clip-clop of hooves and the clink-clank of bottles. Each household on the route had a square of cardboard bearing a large, red "M" to display in a street-facing window when a dairy delivery was wanted. Milk came in quarts, rich cream was bottled by pints and "gills" (a liquid measure amounting to, I believe, a half-pint). Sufficient empties were left on the doorstep or just inside the porch to replace the full ones delivered. In those less crime-ridden days, either cash or prepurchased "milk tickets" were commonly left on the step for the milkman as well. There was no homogenized milk, and the cream in each bottle would rise to the top of the bottleneck. It was generally shaken to blend the constituents before being poured. If left outside or in a cold porch in winter, the contents of the bottle would freeze and expand, producing an icy, extruded cylinder topped by the cardboard bottle top. Many milk-wagon horses knew their routes by heart, and would stop at each customer's house automatically, unless the lack of a cardboard "M" prompted the driver to give the reins a shake and pass the place by.

Bread and coal were also delivered by horse and wagon, but the event that excited small boys most was the arrival of the ice wagon. There were four main ice companies operating out of Dartmouth: Otto's, Chittick's, Hutchinson's and Carter's. They harvested the product each winter from the Dartmouth lakes, and stored it in huge, well-insulated warehouses along the lakeshores. Their wagons were low and heavily built, with the appropriate company name painted along the sides and always dripping a trail of water behind them on the street. There was a seat at the front for the iceman, and a wooden step at the rear where he chipped and chopped the blocks of ice to size. Then he'd grip the ice, weighing upwards of forty pounds, with a pair of tongs and carry it into the customer's house. There, he'd fine-tune the sizing of the block with an ice pick so it would fit the galvanized-iron innards of the icebox. Once paid, he'd put the cash into a battered leather purse that hung from his belt like a sporran, return to the wagon and cluck the horse into a slow walk to the next customer.

That was the moment when we youngsters would jump up on the wagon's back step and ride for a few moments while we reached into the scarred and splintered body of the vehicle and gathered up gleaming shards of refreshing ice on which to suck. Some icemen were unperturbed by this, others would swivel in their seat and growl, "Bugger off, you boys!" It didn't matter much to us either way. To put a hand on us, the driver would have to halt the horse, dismount and come to the back of the wagon, by which time we'd have been well on our way.

Horse-propelled peddlers also drove the streets with their horses and carts in the warmer months selling their wares. Two common commodities were mackerel and bananas, and the hoarse, coarse cries of the peddlers were less than articulate, usually accenting one syllable of their merchandise to the near-exclusion of the others. All you'd hear of mackerel, for instance, was "maaaack," while bananas emerged as "naaan."

Other commercial visitors sometimes came to our door. Among them were knife and scissor sharpeners with a mobile grindstone, fishmongers and sellers of bibles and encyclopaedias. Mi'kmaq basket weavers were occasional visitors, as were ladies from the Preston area on the Dartmouth side who would come with freshly picked mayflowers in season. My mother always bought some, and rhapsodized so expressively over them that the increasingly rare whiff of our official provincial flower still gives me a strong twinge of nostalgia.

During this time motorized deliveries were becoming more common, especially in certain services including laundry and dry cleaning. The latter service was discharged, at least in our area, by a lanky man who'd loudly bawl, "Your friend the dry cleaner!" at the back porch, return the newly cleaned clothing from his last visit, and take possession of any dirty items that had accumulated since.

Phoned-in grocery orders were normally pedalled to customers by delivery boys on bikes built specifically for the job. The back wheel was standard size, but the front was much smaller, leaving room above it for a large basket which could hold a sizable order. As a schoolboy I got a part-time job at the Studley Grocery at the corner of Coburg Road and LeMarchant Street during one pre-Christmas rush. My work, which paid pocket change, was bagging orders, stocking shelves, sweeping the floor and sprinkling fresh sawdust to keep the dust down and soak up blood from the butcher's block. The real excitement came when, once or twice, I was given the chance to bike an order out to someone in the neighbourhood.

I can still remember the absolute delight that came at the end of my brief tenure. It was Christmas Eve and Bill Mason, the youngish proprietor of the store, had the door locked a little before regular closing time. He went from one employee to the next handing out Christmas bonuses. As a temporary employee I didn't really expect one, but when he came to me Bill placed a dollar bill in my hand and thanked me for my help. It was crisp and new, looking as though it had just rolled off the presses of the Royal Canadian Mint. To the best of my memory, it was the first folding money I ever put in my pocket. I skipped home through gathering darkness amid a light sprinkling of snow feeling like King Midas himself.

11

Radio

RADIO, IN MY YOUTH, WAS big. Very big. It encompassed mystery, glamour, science. It was at the leading edge of modernity, the very word invoking a New Age. There were small-town restaurants called the Radio Café. A popular little red wagon for children was the Radio Flyer. There was even a brand of tinned peas called Radio. Whole shops, such as Bligh's on Quinpool Road, were devoted only to the sale and repair of radios.

Until I was about nine years old, the only Halifax station was CHNS. Before I was born, the studios of that budding station were located in the Carleton Hotel on Argyle Street: thus the call sign, standing for "Carleton Hotel Nova Scotia." Their next home was in another hotel, the Lord Nelson. By the time I was nine, the station had moved into a vacant church on Tobin Street that had been done over in art deco style and dubbed Broadcasting House.

During the thirties and forties one favourite personality of Halifax kids (at least, those lucky enough to have family radios) was Uncle Mel. In real life he was Hugh Mills of the Mills Brothers clothing store on Spring Garden Road. When his pre-suppertime show was on, my friends and I could usually be found with the *Halifax Mail* newspaper spread out on our living room rugs as we followed the reading of the comic page by Uncle Mel. I don't quite know why this was considered such a treat by kids who were perfectly capable of reading the comics themselves, but it was. I can still hear that avuncular voice on our Rogers Majestic saying, "And then, in the next picture, we see Popeye swallowing a can of spinach and then saying to Olive Oyl, "I yam what I yam and tha's all that I yam."

The commercials on that show were mostly for local products like Schwartz Peanut Butter, "Say Schwartz and be sure" and Maple Leaf Dairy, with its jingle: "Maple Leaf, Maple Leaf, that's the milk for me, ev'ry day I drink it for my breakfast, lunch and tea!"

Other CHNS regulars were chatty Anna Dexter, who conducted a morning women's program, Major William Borrett with his history program, *Tales Told Under the Old Town Clock*, and the indescribably boring Dr. H.L. Stewart, a Dalhousie professor whose Sunday afternoon philosophies, though they stunned whole families into a stupor, were listened to as some sort of obligation. The station had its own music director, Richard Fry, whose stylings on the juicy-toned Hammond organ graced many a show. Local hero Hank Snow was heard both live and on Bluebird records. School kids gave choral recitals on *Your Children Sing* and an early school competition was *I.Q. Tournament (The Interschool Quiz)*. I was on the LeMarchant Street School team in grade nine. The quiz was conducted with the four-member teams in separate studios, each with its own quizmaster and the same set of questions. The quizmasters were John Funston, who was, I believe, the chief announcer at CHNS, and Jimmy Tapp, a fledgling broadcaster who went on to greater things with CBC, CJAD, Montreal and other stations.

Haligonian Hank Snow "on the air."

By that time some friends and I had already been on the *Uncle Mel* show to present Mr. Mills with a five dollar donation to the Queen's Canadian Fund in aid of air-raid victims in London. The sum was raised, as I recall, by selling home-crafted leather key tags to a market entirely limited to neighbours and family. I'd also sung on the air in a Christmas concert with the boys' choir of the Cathedral of All Saints, warbling "Once in Royal David's City" and some other carols.

For all the allure of CHNS, some of the most exotic fare was to be pulled in on the aforementioned Rogers Majestic radio. This cathedral-like wooden wonder included the broadcast band on which a boy could dial up American AM stations, as well as all sorts of international shortwave stations. It featured "Magic Eye" tuning, a small, early version of a cathode ray tube. When a station was properly tuned, a wide V-shape on the cool green circle sharpened into an acute angle.

To hear the plummy accent of a BBC announcer intone, to the chimes of Big Ben, "This is London calling," was to be transported to the heart of an Empire at war. I always fancied the loud cracks of static were the sounds of an air raid right outside the studio. Another close to home reminder of the world conflict was the daily, late afternoon announcement, "Attention all lightkeepers Atlantic Coast. Please carry out instructions A for Apple." The instruction was repeated in French, with the A standing for Alphonse. I had no idea what the mysterious instruction implied, but imagined that some lights were to remain dark to avoid giving guidance to enemy submarines.

Either by transcriptions from CHNS or direct from their source, the weekly evening shows were not to be missed. There was a good menu of spooky stuff, including *The Shadow*, *The Whistler*, *Inner Sanctum* and *The Weird Sisters*. Popular movies were adapted for Lux Radio Theater, and usually featured top Hollywood stars performing live before a studio audience. The series was hosted by the great film director Cecil B. DeMille himself.

Edgar Bergen, Jack Benny, Bob Hope and Fred Allen ran the top comedy shows, and adventure fare included *The Green Hornet*, *Big Town* and the all-Canadian series *L for Lanky*, featuring a fictional Lancaster bomber and its crew. The favourite of all these stirring offerings was, of course, *The Lone Ranger*, during which somebody was bound to ask, "Who was that masked man?" As someone has observed, it takes a truly cultured old person to hear the *William Tell Overture* and *not* think of that beloved show.

Singin' Sam the Coca Cola Man was a popular afternoon show, as were the ubiquitous soap operas like *Pepper Young's Family*, *Ma Perkins* and *The Right to Happiness*, along with the Canadian-produced *Laura Limited*. A lighthearted daily noontime show from Toronto was *The Happy Gang*. It was so loved by school kids that it was counted as great compensation for being sick at home and able to catch it. All in all, the richness of radio before the days of "formula" programming was immense.

There came a day when I, like most of my buddies, was prompted to acquire a radio so I could listen in bed. How did we manage to acquire our very own sets? Easy. We made them. All it took was a toilet paper tube, some coil wire to wrap around it, a twenty-five-cent lead sulphide crystal the size of a ju-jube, a "cat's whisker" of wire coiled into a tiny spring with a quarter-inch tail and an earphone or discarded telephone receiver. Much to most parents' dismay, an antenna was strung out the bedroom window, connected to a porcelain "lightning arrester" (which we boys mistakenly believed offered absolute safety from a strike) and thence to the tiny, cigar-box-mounted set. Finally a ground wire was attached to the bedroom radiator — another annoyance to the adults — and you were in business. No house current, no tubes, no speaker, no great volume. Just a Rube Goldberg kind of apparatus that employed scrounged, or at least cheap, parts to bring the world to one's bedside.

The rig worked by twitching the cat's whisker's tip around the rough surface of the crystal until you encountered a sweet spot, where the faint signal of a local station came through. On school nights it was risky to sneak the earphone under the blankets, because a checkup by one's mother made discovery inevitable. But on Friday night, it was different: a blind parental eye was turned, and one was free to pick up the *Friday Night Fights*, brought to you "by Gillette Blue Blades — with the sharpest edges ever honed." In retrospect it seems an unlikely sport to interest a skinny kid who'd never actually seen a boxing match and didn't know a jab from an uppercut. But it was live, it was from a far-off location (either Madison Square Garden or St. Nicholas Arena in New York) and it had a regular cast of characters who could be counted on to keep one awake and alert. The announcers were Don Dunphy, whose staccato delivery provided the blow-by-blow, and Bill Corum, whose commentary always ended, "There's the bell, here's Don." The referee was usually Ruby Goldstein, and to get the whole sound spectacle started, there was the call, "and now, with our national anthem, Miss Gladys Gooding!" The ringside doctor appointed by the New York State Boxing Commission was also introduced, and the fight was on.

As time went on, the haywire contraption with the coil and crystal was retired (though the ugly, sagging aerial still dangled from my bedroom windowsill). Then, just before the advent of television, I myself grew up and became, first, an occasional vocal recitalist and later a staff radio announcer at CBC, initially at CBI Sydney and later in Halifax.

I've always remembered what the radio drama producers of those times used to say: "Radio plays beat television plays any day. Why? Because the pictures are better."

There's still something to that.

12

Tracks

IN THE SOUTH END OF Halifax, there was no "wrong side of the tracks." The railway channel that was blasted through bedrock between Rockingham and the present waterfront yards early in the twentieth century ran through sumptuous estates on either side. Despite this intrusion, the properties bisected by the chasm retained their upscale nature, and residents got accustomed to the railway traffic that chuffed through their neighbourhood day and night. There were, of course, the workaday freights with their long succession of boxcars, flatcars and hoppers. They moved the bulk of Canada's commercial cargoes from coast to coast in a day when the eighteen-wheeler rig was yet to be conceived.

The local lines included the Halifax and Southwestern, which ran to Yarmouth down the South Shore and the Dominion Atlantic which reached the same destination via the Annapolis Valley and the Fundy shore. The nationwide CNR line was the one that linked Halifax with the cosmopolitan and cowboy-country attractions of the west.

In any case, to our little gang of boys, "down the tracks" was a rock-walled world of our own, far more interesting than the well-kept real estate on either side. Of course, every visit we made was technically trespassing, given that the right-of-way was well-decorated with warning signs to that effect. But never did we get chased off during the four or five years the "cut" was our favourite destination after school. How clearly I remember scuttling home after the 3:30 pm discharge from LeMarchant Street School, kicking open the front door of our Dalhousie Street home, slinging my schoolbag into the porch and running the short block to the Oakland Road bridge.

There we'd gather, an ever-changing mix of South End adventurers. The expedition might include Bud, Woo, Ducker, Scratchy, Hess, Gumpy, Buddy and a number of other young lads. The quorum of the day would scramble down the rocky cliff to the bottom and head south toward the terminals. The walk was a mixed routine of teetering along the steel rails, hopping from cross tie to cross tie, roving the drainage ditches on either side and crunching through the gravel ballast. The latter footing was always a bit dodgy because of the primitive sewage disposal system in use in the passenger cars of the time. Passengers did their business in the cramped cubicle provided in each car, then pulled a chain or trod on a pedal, emptying the surplus substances directly onto the roadway beneath. These random deposits, though disgusting, were usually avoidable.

As we walked toward the terminal yards, we were always vigilant for something of interest. When there was a scramble for a "find" Woo would keep his place but shout, "I get it if it's any good" — more in hope than expectation. My most prized discovery ever was a broken brakeman's kerosene lantern that I kept for several years in our cellar, my parents having expressed a reluctance (unreasonable, I felt) to display it on the mantel upstairs. We'd also snag the occasional signal flare that had been snuffed before it was totally burnt out or a paperback that had been tossed away from a passenger car. Now and then we'd spot a "track bomb" about the size of a fig newton clipped to the rail as a signal to the following train, but we steered clear of those. The omniscient Woo had informed us that we'd surely cause a major train wreck if we removed the device, and also that it contained a powerful explosive called fulminate of mercury. That was enough to warn us off, but it was an exotic sighting (and something I expect very few people younger than I will have encountered).

Other finds included brochures dropped from Canadian troop trains graphically detailing not the pleasures of sex but the immense bother of sexually transmitted diseases. Perhaps our most exciting haul came on the afternoon we boarded an unoccupied passenger train on a siding only to discover a scattering of dog-eared magazines and rumpled newspaper pages. Normally, such items wouldn't warrant a second look, but these prizes were printed in German. We were on a vacated prisoner of war train, and we were in absolute awe. Here we had, in our little Canadian hands, stuff that had actually been in the hands of real German soldiers. The enemy! The very foes frequently demonized by Prime Ministers Winston Churchill and MacKenzie King! As youngsters woefully ignorant of the real nature of war but captivated by the adventure of the whole thing, this kindled a fever in our imaginations. The very air seemed impregnated with the breath of Jerries. Huns. *Nazis*!

There's one event, though, that eclipsed even the troop train excursion. That was the afternoon a dirty, stubby yard engine came labouring down the tracks behind us. We yelled at the engineer to give us a ride, mostly as a spontaneous reflex. To our amazement, the grubby little locomotive hissed and squealed to a stop, and the friendly driver called, "Jump aboard, boys." We could hardly believe it: this was heaven. The drive was only two or three bridges long, but we relished the beast's steam, coal dust, flame, smoke and noise right at the source. We watched the red coals glowing in the firebox. We felt, through the soles of our feet, the wheels clacking over the joints of the tracks. We were railroaders, thundering toward Montreal in the cab of the Ocean Limited or steaming through the Deep South on the Dixie Flyer! Well, it seemed so, and that engagement of all a youngster's keen senses is still at the forefront of my memory, and all thanks to the grimy engineer of a drab little shunter.

The real beauties among locomotives belonged to the noble 6000 series of steam engines, most powerful Canadian engines of their time. Magnificent and sleek, they pulled the fastest, most elite CNR passenger trains. Like the automobile makes we had each declared entitlement to as they passed, each of us had a 6000 locomotive of his "own." When one of these passed as we strolled the tracks, it was a big moment: "Hey! That's my engine!" It probably silly of me to now claim mine as 6034, but it's the number that seems to stick in my mind these many years since.

Other choice sightings were the hand trolleys that clattered past with track crew members pumping the handles on the way to a job, or one of the diesel jitney cars that carried commuters to and from the Bedford district. The engines of these produced a percussive bark that led us to dub the conveyance "Fartin' Annie." In winter we saw the occasional plow bursting through snow-drifts. The plows, pushed by a locomotive, looked like a caboose with a pointed front end and made a spectacular show if the snow was deep.

Now and then we'd see a brakeman nonchalantly walking the roof of a slow freight boxcar. Some distance before each bridge, there were gallows-like structures with dangling ropes that would brush such daredevils, reminding them to duck. We'd also watch as yardmen walked along the right-of-way refilling containers of caustic soda that I think was used to clear switches of ice. We didn't need Woo to steer us clear of that stuff.

I've said that we were never kicked off the right-of-way itself, but there was an occasion when three of us got in serious trouble from a position on the Oakland Road bridge. Gumpy, Hess and I were leaning over the railing, pinging stones off the roofs of some boxcars passing beneath. Stupid, yes, but such activities were the way boys of our time and place kept boredom at bay. So engrossed were we with our irresponsible task that we failed to notice as a burly man approached. He flashed a badge and introduced himself as a railway policeman, then asked each of us in turn what he was doing. Hess replied that he was throwing his stones at the unoccupied side of the double track. That didn't go down very well, blatant lie that it was. When Gumpy's turn came he explained that he was strafing the rock walls of the cut, nothing more. That too was scorned. Then the railway cop turned to me. Having observed that falsehoods were useless, I admitted to bombarding boxcars. A stern lecture followed, as the constable told us that someone had recently thrown a rock through the window of a passenger car, and he was on assignment to catch the culprit.

Though none of us would ever had done something that destructive and dangerous, the thought that we might even be suspected of such a crime sent a severe jolt of fear through me. It turned out that the railway cop didn't seriously pursue that possibility, but there was indeed to be some retribution for the boxcar pelting. The man asked where we lived. When he learned that each of our homes was a block or so from the bridge, he walked us home, one by one. First stop was Hess's home on Rockcliffe Street, mere steps from the scene of the bust. His Mum answered the door, listened to the charges and told her son to go to his room. There, I later learned, he was commanded to write a hundred lines: "I will not throw stones at trains." Next stop was Gumpy's house, with me still in tow. There was a similar disclosure to his mother, and he was hauled into the house with a scowl.

Then up Dalhousie Street we went, my custodian and I. As we neared the house at the corner I could see my father, out in the driveway washing the family car. He turned off the hose at our approach and listened with obvious concern as the big man showed his badge and explained the circumstances. As he wound up his account he paused a moment and then said, "I should tell you, sir, of the three boys he was the only one who told the truth." My dad's expression relaxed, just a trifle, as he thanked the officer and ordered me into the house. There I waited for him to finish washing the car, wondering what the punishment was to be. When, finally he came inside, my father didn't say much, let alone punish me severely. He said I'd done wrong, adding that I'd owned up and should never do such a thing again. It was a relief, but for some time I was inwardly questioning myself: what might I have told the policeman I was doing had I been the first one he asked?

Another thing we did from the bridge was dispose of our superannuated model airplanes. Given their erratic flights, these little wood and paper craft, propelled by a twisted rubber band, normally had short lives. When the time came that they were too scuffed, twisted and generally beat up to fly properly, we'd repair to the Oakland bridge with the derelict craft and a small container of banana oil, usually used to "dope" the tissue paper of a model kit to stiffen and seal it. One squirt of oil, a kitchen match and the launch was on. What was supposed to be a spectacular crash and burn was inevitably a fizzle: six or eight seconds of flickering flight and a pathetic shred of sticks and paper at the end. Even so, it seemed a more appropriate end to a flying machine than the family garbage can.

As high school neared and girls entered the picture the tracks gave way to other pursuits. But, though the age of diesel took over the land of steam, smoke and cinders stayed infused in our minds. Mine, at least. There's now but a single track through the cut, the brakeman-warning gallows are gone along with flares, track bombs, oil lanterns and cabooses. The cut is now surrounded by deeded parkland and its rock walls covered with garish graffiti. Win some, lose some.

After high school I became, for three memorable months, a real railwayman. That's if a summer job washing dishes in CN dining cars qualifies me for the term. Of course, that's another memory, which still waits to be mined.

13

Wheels

THE FACT THAT OUR FAMILY had no car for the first nine years of my life did nothing to diminish my interest in the subject. All boys loved cars and knew cars. It was a point of particular honour to be able to tell, at a glance, a Terraplane from a DeSoto, a Studebaker from a Stutz. There were dozens of now-defunct (and virtually all North American) makes running the streets then, in addition to the omnipresent Big Three. There were Franklins and Auburns, Reos, Hupmobiles, Hudsons and Grahams. There was even an ancient McLaughlin in Halifax, with special esteem going to the first kid to spot it. But in our pantheon of autodom, the most glorious motor car of all was not a Lincoln Zephyr or a Cadillac, but the big, sleek, high-styled Packard.

My first close exposure to the make was in 1938 when an easygoing guy named Doug was courting my Aunt Carol. The two had met in Montreal when she was training as a nurse there. He followed her home to Halifax, where one afternoon he offered Carol's gangling nephew (me) a lift in his beautiful dark green Packard convertible...with the top down! We took off, just the two of us, and tooled around the South End for a bit. He was obviously proud of his prize auto and I, in turn, was in absolute ecstasy, craning my neck in all directions to see if anyone I remotely knew saw me as we passed. Sadly, no.

But better was to come. He stopped the car on Oxford Street just south of Coburg and slid me halfway behind the wheel while he maintained control of the gas and brake pedals. Off we went, heading south on the unpaved road, with me at the wheel! It didn't last long, but it was as thrilling as it was illegal. I was a seven-year-old at the wheel of a big, shiny behemoth, with the wind in my hair and a thumping in my chest. Aunt Carol didn't need any prompting when Uncle-to-be Doug popped the question, but that afternoon run had me firmly in his corner.

Later, as the war began, private automobile production slowed and stopped, but we growing boys still had the whole range of prewar cars to admire and identify. And Packard was the Queen of the Fleet. Our reaction to a "spotting" was simple: the first to identify an approaching example was to bellow "PACKARD!" at the top of his voice. No prize, no right to punch anyone on the arm, just the thrill of being the first one to yell out the name of the finest make of car in Halifax.

Other vehicles of note were some of the city works department trucks that were old enough to have solid tires rather than pneumatic. And steamrollers were the real thing: clanking, coal-fired chuffers with a boiler like a locomotive, a tall smokestack, a spinning flywheel along one side and a device called a governor. This provided endless fascination to the youngsters who always gathered to watch a roller at work. It consisted of three table tennis ball–sized spheres of solid brass, each at the end of a hinged metal rod. The faster the engine ran, the farther out from the vertical these weights flew. But as they flew out by centrifugal force, smaller rods hinged at their centre pulled on a collar around the main shaft, just as the ribs of an umbrella pull their central collar up when opened. The more the collar rose, the less steam went to the piston, the balls would drop as they slowed, and the steam feed would increase. This beautifully simple engineering concept was deeply fascinating to me and the others, and every detail of this glorious beast, right down to the water-soaked hemp mat that cleaned the main roller as it turned, is etched in my memory. But I guess you had to be there.

The transfer business in town was largely done by horse and wagon. Many of the wagons operated by such as Adams Transfer and Thompsons were of a peculiar type called slovens: flatbed drays with their axles higher than the low-slung platform, which was only a few inches from the ground. This gave the advantage of easy loading without sacrificing the size of the big, ironclad wheels. As these conveyances clattered along the lower, cobbled streets they created a percussive composition featuring horseshoes, wheel rims and jingling harness. The draymen who ran them (who tended to be rough and ready knockabouts in long leather aprons) added hoarse "giddyups" and "whoas" to the accompaniment. Slovens were a very common part of the Halifax downtown scene, at least up to the start of the war. One wonders where these battered old relics of an ending era went to die.

Other wheels important to kids, then as now, were bicycles. Except, in our day, virtually all "wheels," as we called them, were one-speed. The vast majority were CCMs, a fact that worked to my disadvantage and illustrates the fact that even in that day there were status brands and outcast brands. My first (and only) bike, a birthday present from my parents, was a shiny, black British beauty: a Raleigh. I rode forth proudly on my new steed, only to discover that I was mounted on an import despised and rejected by most other cyclists my age. "Raleigh? What the heck is that? Never heard of it. Geez, don't you know CCM is the only kind?" It renewed my memories of the ridicule I endured with my first (and also only) pair of rollerskates. "What? No ball bearings? Geez, they're no good. . .gotta have ball bearings!"

Among Halifax lads, there were two kinds of bike riders. There were the amateurs like my lot and the true professionals: telegraph boys. These teenaged couriers vanished from our streets after the war, but in their heyday they whizzed around downtown by the dozens, wearing grey uniforms featuring peaked caps, long-sleeved jackets, britches and leather gaiters. Most of them seemed smallish and all seemed tough. While waiting for wires to be delivered, they'd congregate, spitting, smoking and swearing, on Granville Street where both the Canadian Pacific and Canadian Telegraph Companies had their offices. Once despatched, they'd mount up and deliver their yellow paper messages, dodging in and out of traffic, intimidating pedestrians and emitting piercing whistles through their teeth. This signal was preferred to the use of a bicycle bell, serving both as a warning to others and communication when passing their own kind.

The couriers tended to drive stripped-down cycles, free of fenders or trimmings. But, for the average school kid, various accessories were popular, including two interesting kinds of lamps. One ran by acetylene, or calcium carbide. These may still be around as retro curiosities, but they were an obsolescent rarity in my boyhood. I never had one, but the one or two I got to see were fascinating brass contraptions with tanks, tubes and a silvered reflector and lens. You'd load them with carbide "rocks" and water, generate gas by adjusting the water valve to drip slowly onto the carbide, put a match to the gas jet and bingo! You got an intense flame like a welder's torch. Trouble with these gizmos was their extreme crankiness. They would sputter constantly, and often flame out, requiring the rider to stop, fiddle with the regulator, stir the carbide and relight.

The other interesting lamp was driven by a small egg-cup shaped generator that was fastened to one of the forks so that its small, knurled wheel was turned by the sidewall of the tire. The current thus generated went by a pair of wires to a light on the handlebars. Trouble with this rig was that the slower you went, the dimmer the light. Bike stops, light goes out. The lowest-tech lighting system of all, common in my set, was a U-shaped fitting of spring steel that was clamped to the handlebars and, in turn, accepted an ordinary flashlight. None of these systems could hold a candle (no pun) to the array of cheap, high-output electronic marvels available today. Seems a pity so many bicyclists now prefer to ride the streets at night with not so much as a reflector to give motorists a chance to spot them.

In my time, things were tough for bikes: the tramcar tracks used to grab the front wheel, especially on wet days, and either tip you or force you to stop. Unpaved surfaces were littered with small, sharp rocks that would flatten a tire in a wink. And the cobbled streets were slippery when wet and punishing on tires. Bike racks were few, and throwing the machine roughly to the ground on dismounting was common practice.

But our bikes were mostly equal to the punishment, even the Raleigh...at least until my very last stunt. At our summer place I rode down a steep hill with a deep ditch at the bottom, intending to yank up the front wheel at just the right time to clear it. Instead, I chose the wrong time. Smashing into the ditch, I was vaulted over the handlebars. The crash crumpled the front wheel and bent the forks badly. But by that time my beginner's licence was only a couple of years away, and the world of motor cars loomed larger than ever.

14

Entertainment

I WELL REMEMBER MY FIRST exposure to real theatre rather than the homegrown pageants and concerts held in the assembly hall of LeMarchant Street School. It was an amateur production of *The Taming of the Shrew* mounted, as I recall, by the Theatre Arts Guild. The venue was the Dalhousie Gymnasium, built to replace the original gym which had burned to the foundation (some say as a destructive student prank). The new gym was a basic concrete box with a glossy varnished floor marked for basketball, badminton and other indoor games. But (as I was to appreciate when working on the Glee Club stage crew in later years) the stage was almost at a professional level: big dimmer board, flying space, generous wings, thick velvet curtain and all.

I was about eight, and I was awed from the outset by the lavish costumes and period set.

Then, just as I was becoming truly absorbed, came the scene where Petruchio has a fit about a badly cooked roast of beef and throws it to the floor. I had no doubt I was beholding an authentic, juicy sirloin on the platter. But when it hit the floor, there was only a scuffling sound, as the supposed meat hit the stage. Then it

The late, lamented Capitol Theatre.

skipped and bounced several times, spinning in mid-air as no real rump of beef would have done. This was papier maché. . .a fraud! I had yet to learn the principle of willing suspension of disbelief, something my father later explained to me in simple terms. After that, I was converted, and for the rest of my life it has taken a really bad gaffe to spoil my enjoyment of a stage work.

Then, of course, there were the movies, a lightning-fast development on the entertainment scene. My parents were married while "silents" were still running, but by the time I was six the cinema had advanced to the magical level of Walt Disney's Snow White. As we grew into double digits, my buddies and I were permitted more adult fare, and reveled in an abundance of movies, most of the "B" variety. The closest we had to a neighbourhood movie house was the brand new Oxford in all its art

Movies at the Orpheus were worth the wait.

deco elegance. Saturday matinees there featured a one-reel serial along with the main feature, with stars like western idols Johnny Mack Brown, Tex Ritter and Randolph Scott. Each episode left the hero in a dangerous, seemingly inescapable situation that was resolved in the first few frames of next Saturday's segment.

The favourite and finest theatre was the Capitol at the foot of Spring Garden Road, with a portcullis hanging over the stage and a suit of armour in the lobby. A block or so north on Barrington stood the Orpheus, with the Family almost directly across from it. The venerable Garrick was on Sackville just above Barrington. Remembered by my mother as the home of Acker's Family Vaudeville, it was another "B" movie house where we came to enjoy such heroes of the genre as Lon Chaney Jr. and Lex Barker.

I imagine the present Neptune still contains some of the fabric of the compact Edwardian structure.

There was another movie house farther north on Barrington at the corner of Buckingham (now engulfed by Scotia Square). It was the dreaded Gaiety, which, according to South End parents, was a "flea pit" or a "bug farm." It was also in the area we kids considered the tough part of town, so we never chanced a visit. Likewise, such North End houses as the Empire, the Community and the Casino were usually considered too far off our comfortable patch for us.

I was about seven when my maternal grandfather, Will Sandford, opened another entertainment portal for me. The circus came to town, and he took me. It was the Robbins Bros. Circus, and it was a three ringer. The show itself was preceded by a real circus parade on Barrington Street, (possibly the last ever held in our town) and the sidewalks were packed. There were caged tigers, clowns, an elephant, pretty ladies and, at the end, an actual steam calliope spewing white plumes from its bellowing pipes. There can't be too many people left who've heard that sound. That afternoon, Grampy and I found our way to the big top. I must admit my memories have faded somewhat. However, sounds and sights of the classic twelve-clowns-in-a-car routine, trapeze artists and a rather tatty circus band blaring "Entry of the Gladiators" are still with me.

Speaking of bands, Christmas was always made sweeter by the expert Salvation Army ensembles that played on street corners during the season. Then, as World War II began, Haligonians were treated to big military bands of the finest order. The best, in my view, was the Stadacona Band, which often headed naval parades that stretched for many blocks along Barrington Street. There were three or four dozen players, the petty officers with their polished brass buttons, ratings with their "square rig" uniforms: gleaming white cap covers, pipe-clayed gaiters and web belts. Of particular grandeur were the leopard-skin apron of the bass drummer, and the white gauntlets of the tall drum major who twirled the brass-headed baton. When they launched into the navy march past, "Heart of Oak," the effect was heart pumping. Boys like me found it splendid and inspiring, and to us it carried no portent of the bloody misery of combat. Just pomp and glory.

In those days the Lord Nelson Hotel provided regular employment for three local musicians and entertainment for those who strolled through the lobby on Sundays. The group was something of a "palm court" ensemble, consisting of Oscar Welti, Nick Schuster and Marjorie Payne: respectively on violin, cello and piano. They played near the entrance to the elegant dining room.

Near the low end of the cultural scale, but high in entertainment value, was the annual spectacle of the Bill Lynch Greater Exposition Show, held on the corner of the North Common where tennis is played today. This was tawdry glamour! There were lurid sideshow banners depicting acts such as the Lobster Boy. There was the non-stop music emanating from the automated machine near the entrance (which featured robotic drums and cymbals). And the aroma of greasy burgers, gristly hot dogs and fries dripping overused fat created a pretty heady atmosphere. I sometimes wonder if my fascination with the sideshow "talkers" presaged my later employment as a radio announcer. Some of the phrases, distorted by the cheap amplifiers, ring in my head yet: "See the funny little monkeys," "Astonishing freaks of nature," "Riders facing incredible danger on the Wall of Death," "It's no Sunday school picnic, it's red-hot and it's risqué."

Bill Lynch Greater Exposition Shows.

The rides? Piece of cake. There wasn't a Tilt-a-Whirl or a Whip that could make us lose our cookies or a Ferris wheel that could beat the view from the Dingle Tower. The games? I'd have been a sucker for any of them, but our streetwise friend Mop argued that all the games were rigged and that it was fair ball to swindle the swindlers. He enlisted a crony (not me — too frightened by half) and showed him how to lean on his forearms at the counter of the Crown and Anchor game once the wheel had started to turn. When it clicked to a stop, Mop would slide a dime under the assistant's splayed elbow onto a winning square. The confederate would stand up and stroll away as our fearless friend collected his winnings. I also witnessed a midway trick that netted a couple of boys three baseballs at the cost of a quarter. The victim was the operator of the "cat rack," where the stuffed and liberally fringed kitties had to be knocked off the platform (a virtually impossible task). Our trickster friend sent his colleagues outside the fairground to a spot behind the concession. He then paid his quarter for three balls and, instead of aiming at the cats, threw them completely over the game tent where they were caught by the accomplices. All ran off with their ill-gotten booty, but in fact the joke was on them. They didn't net regulation baseballs, but rigged versions weighing much less (the better to avoid a payoff).

Then there was an entertainment that should perhaps be billed as "no-brow": wrestling at the Shirley Street Arena. I don't suspect that many of my chums ever let their parents know about our attendance at these spectacles. But go we did. The rickety building presented a parade of heroes and villains dressed in what looked like wool bathing trunks, and sometimes we chose to annoy those near us by cheering for the bad guys. In fact, on one occasion a testy old lady in the row ahead swung her purse at our group and told us to shut up.

Among the favourites were battlers like "Cowboy" Len Hughes, "Krusher" Al Korman, "Bull" Currie, "Bull" Montana and Dr. John "Dropkick" Murphy. Sometimes celebrities (or ex-celebrities) took over the ring as referees, one of them being Jack Dempsey.

My hero was Murphy, for a particular reason. I'd not only met the man, he and his family had rented the cottage next door to ours during one summer spent at Hubbards. I must have been seven or eight, and had yet to see a match, but the resort area was abuzz about the famous wrestler in our midst. He was a kindly and pleasant man, and the word was that he was a real physician, something I've never been able to verify. But maybe my father believed in his doctoral billing because, when one of my baby teeth became loose, he suggested that I approach the great man and ask him to do the extraction. I asked, timidly and he agreed, genially. With one deft pull of his muscular fingers, my tooth was ready to put under my pillow. I told the story more than once, but I don't think any of my schoolmates ever believed it.

Back to the top-of-brow range, I well remember my first exposure to live symphonic music, though it was a far cry from the wealth of classical concerts available today. I was in my teens and a voice student at the Maritime Conservatory of Music. The director of the Conservatory was the late Ifan Williams, a Welsh immigrant to Canada who did more than anyone or anything else to make the institution what it is today. He decided that there were sufficient students on hand to make up not a full symphony, but a fair-sized chamber equivalent. His choice for the debut was Mozart's Symphony No. 41, the *Jupiter*, and every time I hear its strains I recall how it sounded in the dusty premises of the Conservatory, then housed at the corner of Summer Street and Spring Garden Road.

And that, to my recollection, was when the balance started to tip. New immigrants, notably from Latvia, brought seedlings of European culture to our town. There was Mariss Vetra, a former director of the Latvian National Opera, who came to teach voice at the old Conservatory and who conducted the fledgling Nova Scotia Opera Association. There was Alfred Strombergs and his wife Hilda, he a conductor who formed the chamber orchestra the Halifax Symphonette and she a dancer and choreographer. Juris Gotshalks and his wife Irene Apine founded the Gotshalks Halifax ballet company. Teodor Brilts, another Latvian from Riga, succeeded Vetra at the Conservatory to teach voice. Of all these seminal influences on the local classical scene, only Brilts was to stay here for the rest of his professional life but all of them breathed new life into Halifax culture.

About this time there was an upsurge in jazz and swing music in Halifax. There'd always been plenty of good dance bands, but leaders like Les Single and Lloyd Peach brought new virtuosity to the scene. The kingpin orchestra leader of the day was Don Warner, a young ex-RCAF pilot who had survived a crash landing on a Spanish beach, followed by internment. No day job for Don: he was a bandleader and, later, radio jazz host all his life. He spent a good deal of his income buying new, custom arrangements from Ontario arrangers like Eddie Graf and Pat Riccio, and sometimes even big-name New Yorkers. His standout venue was the Med-O Club at Beechville, a mecca for those who liked tasty music (and a taste of lemon gin from a bottle in a paper bag). Though a serious jazz and swing man, Warner catered, perhaps once per set, to the fun-loving crowd with his popular novelty numbers, some of which involved funny hats. These included "We Hate Singers," "The Preacher and the Bear" and "The Maharajah of Magadore" (he had rubies and pearls and the loveliest girls, but he didn't know how to do the rumba). They always got a big hand.

By that time my boyhood was behind me, but the entertainments of our city were on an upsurge that never ended. Today, as an octogenarian, I marvel at what's available in the auditoriums, clubs, stadiums, stages, bars and bandstands of Halifax. It's become what my teenage mind imagined New York might be like. But, to me, the beauty of it is that mine was the generation that saw the wonderful transformation in my home-town take place.

15

Diversions

AN OLD SONG TELLS US that the best things in life are free, and in the age before the internet, text messaging, iPods, cell phones and their expensive kin, kids of my vintage could certainly find ways galore to divert ourselves at no cost whatever. Portable phones were easy: two tin cans and a ball of string, and voila, instant walkie talkie. Really worked, too, within the limit of the string. Computer games? Well we had an analogue equivalent called tiddly. A piece of old broom handle about five inches long and sharpened at the ends was what you needed. That and a longer stick with which to hit the short one on the end, sending it spinning into the air. Then the game was to keep it in the air as long as you could. I forget how (or even if) score was kept, but unlike chairbound electronic pursuits, it kept more than your fingers moving.

Another simple (though somewhat stupid) amusement was "conkers," which only required a chestnut and eighteen inches of string. It took much searching under a chestnut tree to find the shiniest and plumpest of its progeny. Then, with immense care, you drilled a hole through the middle, threaded the string through and knotted it. Shine it up a bit on your sleeve, and there was your conker, ready for battle. Why battle? Because the objective was to find another kid with a conker, whereupon one boy held his still at the end of its string while the other swung his conker at it with as much skill and force as he could marshal, with the hope of smashing the stationary nut into pieces. If that didn't happen, it was turnabout. The loser was often brought to tears. I told you it was stupid.

Street hockey was more prevalent than today, partly because cars were far fewer. It wasn't free, but the cost ended with the purchase of a hockey stick. The blade of which would be soon worn to a sliver from the friction involved. Shin pads were improvised from old magazines or catalogues. The "puck" was, as often as not, either a worn out tennis ball or one of the hard-frozen horse buns that littered the wintry streets of Halifax in the thirties. I didn't take to the game, principally because every time I got my stick on the Percheron poop, someone bigger and more agile took it away from me. I considered that no fun at all, and it presaged a lifelong lack of athletic aptitude.

But there were other, less strenuous (and fully gratis) diversions to compensate. One could take a fresh alder stick, tap the bark with the handle of a pocket knife until it slid off intact, carve an airway into the wood and have a pretty effective whistle for your efforts. Slingshots were something we pretty well all tried, using a forked stick and a piece of inner tube. Accuracy-wise, they never worked as well as expected, but with a little bad luck they'd break a window handily. For a while, my set favoured a sling like that with which David slew Goliath: long cords, a leather pouch and a smooth pebble. Again, we couldn't slay so much as a barn door, but the carry was great. A rubber band, a wooden spool and two matchsticks could become a self-propelled "tank" that could make its way across a school desk (until it was confiscated). A pocket comb and a square of toilet paper yielded a serviceable kazoo. A spring clothespin and a couple of the inevitable rubber bands, and you had yourself a paperclip pistol. A discarded fedora with the brim removed and the crown cut out in diamonds, circles and hearts yielded a hat just like the one Jughead wore in Archie Comics. A pop bottle cap became a pretty neat badge when you pried out the cork liner then pressed it back into the cap with your shirt pocket in between. A hollowed-out acorn, a paper drinking straw and some tea leaves provided a pipe that would really smoke (and scorch the skin off your tongue to boot). And the simplest free plaything of all was a wide blade of grass, which could be stretched between your thumbs and blown through, emitting a reedy, banshee-like squeal.

Some of the best fun was to be had after supper, when the neighbourhood games began. In my case there were many choices of venue. Three doors up South Street (where Dalplex now stands) was the Burns property, which had a big front yard and a big field behind the house. Across the street were the grounds of the Studley Quoit Club, used for that gentlemanly sport only on weekends. And the adjoining women's residence of Dalhousie, Shirreff Hall, was surrounded by spacious, close-clipped lawns.

The games themselves were many, with the predictable Tag and Hide and Seek augmented by Red Line, Please May I (also known as Giant Steps), Dot the Icebox, Red Rover, Kick the Can and something that we called Oyster Sails, probably a corruption of Hoist Your Sails. Teams were usually chosen through the old "one potato, two potato, three potato, four" procedure. These games had flexible, much-argued-about rules and passed the hours of spring and summer evenings until parents began to call home their representatives on the roster. One mother had the distinctive cry "Coo-ooey" for her kids (which always seemed to me close to the generic call for swine). Others called out the proper names, stringing out the main vowel, as in "Baaaaar-bra" in a falling two-note arrangement. I don't know if the last one called felt privileged or unwanted, because it was never me.

If most of the after-supper games were gender equal, the girls had hopscotch and skipping to themselves. These always began as if ordained by some synchronized city-wide master schedule on some fine day in spring. Stubs of chalk came out and sidewalks began to bear the single and double squares with numbers, providing the "course." The other requirement was a piece of stone, which, as I recall, was moved about, always marking a square where no foot was allowed to fall. The skipping, whether singles or doubles, was usually done to breathless chants. There was, "I am a Girl Guide dressed in blue / These are the actions I must do." There was "Engine, Engine, Number Nine / Going down Chicago line." Also "I am a Pretty Little Dutch Girl" and the slightly shocking "Ann and Bobby sitting in a tree / K-I-S-S-I-N-G" with great emphasis on the second "I."

Marbles (or, more commonly, alleys) were popular, and started about the same time as tiddly, hopscotch and skipping. It was generally a big kid who began the season by digging his heel into the hard-packed ground of the schoolyard and circling around it until there was a usable depression, or hole. By the end of school, there were many such, with some in particular favour because of their dimensions and plenty of clear ground in front. There were plain alleys, large ones called double centres and the little pee-wees, which, for some reason, were the most highly prized. Here again, what rules there may have been are long disremembered, but there were only two forms of the game. One was "keepsies," in which winners actually got to take home the alleys of the losers. The other, despised and scorned by good players, let the contestants leave with their own alleys after the game.

Our first encounter with racy show-biz folk came when the young yo-yo "champions" from the Cheerio company came around to the school at recess. Of course these things weren't free or even cheap, and their demonstrators created a huge yearning in all boys to possess one. They attracted a gathering of school kids the moment they appeared on the grounds. Out came the yo-yos and the spiel began, accompanied by dazzling tricks: sleep, walk the dog, loops, two yo-yos at once, the whole tenor of the presentation subtly centred on the contention that the only spinner that would elevate you to real eminence in the world of yo-yos was the most expensive. Later on, the Bo-lo bat, with its tethered ball, sent champs to the schoolyards to do the same shilling for their product. All these teenage pitchmen were objects of great esteem and celebrity, at least from the time they appeared to when they left, leaving us wondering what enchanted background led them to their stardom.

The letdown, at least in my case, came after I scrimped up enough coinage to buy one of these spectacular instruments only to discover that it was all I could do to make a yo-yo come back to my palm. The dog wouldn't walk, the baby wouldn't rock and the spinner wouldn't sleep.

At least I could coax a really good screech out of a blade of grass. Still can, in fact.

16

The Northwest Arm

OUR HOUSE WAS ONLY TWO blocks down South Street from salt water. The Northwest Arm was much more accessible to the public during my childhood, and my young friends and I took full advantage. We thought nothing of walking along the shoreline from the foot of Oakland Road all the way out to Point Pleasant Park. Most, if not all, of the properties on the east side of the Arm included water lots extending a hundred feet westward, which meant that even when walking below the high tide mark we were trespassing. We, of course, were unaware of that, and it wouldn't have bothered us much if we'd known. We considered the whole outdoors our own. In fact I only recall one instance where a homeowner shouted at us to clear off, which advice we were ready and able to ignore.

The trip along the shore involved clambering over or around various jetties and boathouses, including a stoutly built structure called Senator's Wharf. We'd congregate there for hours, and we even used to skinny dip from it in broad daylight, risking not only charges for indecent exposure but typhoid fever or worse from the nearby sewage outfall.

My neighbourhood, Northwest Arm included.

Another landmark along that shore was the ruins of the old
Nova Scotia Penitentiary, located near the foot of present-day
Inglewood Drive. The big prison had been closed after Con-
federation when federal penitentiaries were established. It had
since served, among other things, as a scrapyard and an electri-
cal generating station, but by the time of our ramblings it was a
totally abandoned rubble of cut stone. There was a hook-shaped
iron rod protruding from a piece of wall, and it didn't take much
boyish imagination for us to see it as a gallows or gibbet, from
which our inward eye could discern hanged convicts dangling
with bulging eyes and kicking legs. In fact, it was likely nothing
but an exposed building truss.

As World War II went on, the walking became much more

difficult. The rocks became covered with a thick layer of bunker oil that had either escaped from torpedoed ships or been pumped from bilges as convoys passed Point Pleasant. The slime-coated rocks were filthy and treacherous, but negotiable by nimble lads. One of the rewards of our beachcombing was the occasional discovery (well, at least twice) of US Army K-Rations washed ashore. These packages of field meals were about the size of a brick, and made from heavily waxed cardboard. On the inside, treasure untold! I remember canned cheese with ham, biscuits, candies and, best of all, chewing gum. In those war years the only chewable confectionery available in stores was spruce gum, sold in small square packages of five birthday candle–sized sticks. In fact, the stuff was no different from what we could pry off local conifers for free, and we disdained it. But this was the real Wrigley, packaged in foil wrap within paper sleeves, just as re-membered from earlier days.

With much argument about fairness, all these goodies were shared and enjoyed. Last came the distribution of the four cig-arettes in the kit, lit with the book of matches that was also provided. Yes, unfortunately we were all used to sneaking smokes despite our youth, and these were real American ciggies, none of your Canadian brands like Players, Turret or Sweet Caporal. They were "enjoyed" with much coughing, some dizziness and a degree of nausea.

We sometimes resorted to another snack found along the shore: periwinkles (always called pennywinkles by us and other youngsters). Oil-free ones could be found in the northern reach-es of the Arm, where we'd harvest handfuls. The next step was to find a not too rusty tin can and some dry twigs and sticks for a fire. Matches were no problem. We always had kitchen matches in our pockets as a virtual necessity of life. (Even after a personal calamity — sitting on a rock with a fresh pocketful of matches in my back pocket — I resumed carrying them before my blistered buttocks were healed).

Once the Arm water was boiling in the tin, in went the winkles. Someone would have a safety pin or straight pin, and when the little gastropods were considered done, we used it to pick the tiny morsels out. Knowing I was under scrutiny, I always managed to consume one or two with feigned delight, but in those days my appetite was notoriously picky, and (to be disgustingly honest) a pin-skewered winkle reminded me of a freshly discovered booger. Thus, I always generously insisted that the others have a bigger share. But when the tiny meal was done, we were all left with the feeling that we were noble foragers living off the bounty of the wild.

In summertime, the boat clubs flourished. They included the Waegwoltic, the Jubilee, St. Mary's and the one to which our family belonged, The Northwest Arm Rowing Club. Like the others, it had many dozens of rowboats, canoes and shells stored in sheds and launched via rollers on the ramps that ran down from the deck to the water. We had a bit of a rivalry with the "Waeg" kids, who had a fancy diving tower and who we considered somewhat snooty. They stung us with their treatment of our NWARC acronym, which they translated as Not Worth a Red Cent. In fact a cent would go a long way at the club canteen, where hard hats, bull's eyes, honeymoons and the like were on sale, along with five cent pop and ice cream cones.

But the real gourmet destination on the Arm was Ken's Canteen on the other side near the tower. Ken and his wife presided in gleaming whites behind the counter and beneath a sign that read,

"The Hot Dog with a Reputation." The rep was well-deserved. The frankfurters were hot, juicy and delicious. The warm, moist buns steamed to perfection. An expertly applied wavy line of mustard, and heaven was in your hand! The cost? The same as the ferryboat fare: five cents. Another nickel, if you had one, bought a play on the Coney Island pinball machine. Ken had the "tilt" mechanism adjusted so that it was relatively easy to beat, and paid off in free games, not money. There was also a Wurlitzer jukebox — another nickel's worth. When you deposited a coin and selected a tune, everybody along the Arm benefited (or suffered, depending on taste) as the music wafted out from a loudspeaker on the canteen roof. Once the nickels were gone, we lads would likely amble up the hill to the Memorial Tower. It offered two diversions. One was mounting the back of one of the two bronze lion sculptures that flanked the doorway. On a hot day the ride would have to be brief, given that the beasts' smooth backs were hot enough to sizzle a hamburger, let alone skinny legs clad in shorts. The other pastime of the area was climbing the tower steps, a giddy experience for vertigo-prone people like me. Once at the top, out would come the ever-present matches. When dropped, one by one, to the concrete sidewalk below they'd light with a satisfying snap. Irresponsible, to be sure, but we at least made sure there were no strollers below.

In winter, the Arm offered the seasonal sport of jumping from one to another of the floating ice pans near the shore. Dangerous? Yes. Daunting? Not to adolescent "immortals." The Arm would pretty much always freeze over in those years. Skaters and even sail-driven iceboats would skitter up and down the surface unless it became ridged, snow-covered or slushy. Boutilier's ferry ran from the foot of Oakland to a wharf near the Memorial

Tower, using a one-cylinder open motorboat in summer and a clinker-built rowboat in winter. The rowboat's passage was frequent enough to maintain a narrow lane of open water, a fact that led to one of the greatest adventures of my entire boyhood.

My Rockcliffe Street friend David Hess and I were puttering about near the ferry wharf one winter's day in wartime when we spotted a sailor trudging over the ice toward the mouth of the Arm. He was in full uniform, including bell-bottom trousers and heavy blue wool greatcoat. He also had a pretty full load aboard, revealed by his wavering gait. He showed no signs of stopping as he approached the ferry path, which was full of floating slush and looked, at first glance, much like the solid ice on either side. David and I hollered shrilly at him, but to no avail.

The inevitable happened: down went Jack Tar, greatcoat and all, into the icy brine. We two, as faithful readers of the *Boy Scout Handbook*, knew exactly what young stalwarts were supposed to do in cases like this. We fetched a long pole from among the driftwood of the shore and pushed it out over the thick ice until we could extend it across the breach. The sailor was able to drag himself out, and came wobbling ashore to where David and I waited to be thanked and praised as heroes right out of an adventure comic. Jack did no such thing. He barked a few curse words toward no one in particular, and sloshed away eastward up Oakland Road (pausing only to throw up into the gutter) and was seen no more. With him he took our anticipated status as civic idols, Royal Humane Society medalists and recipients of Navy League honours. Disillusioned, we trudged off home from our Northwest Arm playground.

17

Tramcars

PUBLIC TRANSIT IN HALIFAX HAS taken several forms from early horsecars to today's diesel buses. My friends and I were lucky enough to grow up in the era of the Birney car, a lightweight electric streetcar that pretty well covered the city from Richmond in the north to Point Pleasant in the south. They were of a single-bogey, or single-truck design, meaning that the vehicle rode on one set of four close-set wheels centered underneath. As a result, the cars would sway and pitch while running, with the bogey as a pivot.

The cars were double-ended so that they could reverse at the end of a line by hauling down and securing the active trolley pole and raising the one at the opposite end to rest its grooved end on the overhead wire. Then the operator would detach his control handles, walk to the "new" front end of the car while swinging the seat backs to face in the opposite direction, install the handles in their sockets and be ready to drive off in the opposite direction. Another fixture, this one installed in the floor of each end, was a round iron trap door lid about the size of a salad plate. There was a flange on the hinge side which lifted the disc when stepped on. We never knew exactly what it was for, but the majority guess was that it allowed the operator to spit onto the tracks rather than onto the flooring. After all, this was the age of chewing tobacco. The bell was also a foot-operated device, a simple iron plunger next to the supposed spit-hole. Interestingly, the fare system was "pay as you leave," which could lead to a problem for people who boarded only to discover they lacked a ticket (three rides for a quarter back then) or silver change.

Despite running on electricity, the Birneys were noisy beasts, especially when cornering. This was because the axles, unlike those of automobiles, were of a piece with the wheels at either end, meaning that when the car negotiated a curve the outer wheels wanted to go faster and the inner wheels slower which, of course, was impossible. So the inner wheel, rather than slow down, spun against the track emitting a horrendous squeal at each corner. Though no engineer, I suspect this resulted in wear on both the track and the wheels. Another sound passengers would periodically hear was that of the air compressor which (even when the car was stationary) produced a sporadic *yung-a-yung-a-yung* noise from underneath. And the trams gave off a pungent smell, more noticeable from outside than inside the tram. This, one learned, was ozone, generated by the electric traction motors.

Although details of the cars' interior fittings varied depending on when they were manufactured, most of the seats were wicker-backed and most of the looped straps for standees were clad in a shiny, ivory-coloured material. There were rolling signs over the ends of the roof to indicate what numbered route the car was on: Windsor-Inglis (7), Agricola-South Park (8), Belt Line (1&2), Armdale (5), Oakland (6), Richmond (3). After dark, this

Downtown with the beloved Birneys.

information was augmented by coloured lights on the roof.

We boys were quite attached to the trams and their motormen. There were certain drivers we revered, including "Chummy" Lawlor, a member of the famous Allen Cup–winning Halifax Wolverines hockey team and Ralph Kemp, a handsome guy who always had a grin and a few words for youngsters on his car. Another was a motorman whose name was Mombourquette (which we shortened to "Mombie"). Harold Snider was yet another affable motorman, who eventually left the tramway service to found Halcraft Print with partner Leo Arakelian, brother of my close friend Armen. Imagine a city so close-knit that kids and public transit drivers could be on first-name terms. (This despite a sign above the motorman's head that read: "Traffic demands operator's full attention. Please do not speak to him.")

The No. 6 line was notable in that it began and ended at the junction of Oakland Road and what is now Beaufort. There, the trolley poles were swapped and the seatbacks reversed, a job often allowed to be done by youngsters. Once the controls were installed at the other end, the car was ready to roll northward. When it got to Oxford and Coburg, there was a switch in the tracks to allow the car to join the Belt Line route and head east. It was operated with a long iron pry bar, and certain operators would allow a young male passenger to do the job, a task that brought a great measure of self-importance with it.

There was a small wooden shelter for waiting passengers at the No. 6, or "Dingle" stop which, when very young, we dirty little boys would employ as a pissoir on occasion. (Well, it beat running all the way home for the sake of a wee sprinkle.) This was a matter of great agitation for the resident of a nearby home, one Captain Atwood, a retired British master mariner. When his navigator's eye discerned or even imagined any leakage on our part, he would come to his door and bellow at us in plummy English tones. We, of course, paid no attention to anyone we could outrun. But there came a day when the enraged seafarer issued a horrifying ultimatum. "If I catch you young buggers peeing in that car-house one more time," he thundered, "I shall come over there and. . ." He then detailed a retribution involving the severance of a cherished body part. Thereafter, shuddering at the thought of the horrifying threat, we resorted to shrubbery out of the captain's view.

The trams, after dark, were subject to various pranks carried out by boys, especially along the block between Chestnut and Lilac Street, across from the Dal campus. There was a car stop in the centre of that block, and the trick was for one boy to wait there as if he wished to board the next car. His cronies would be hiding in a nearby driveway, and when the tram stopped for the supposed passenger, the other lads would scuttle out of their hiding place and pull down the trolley pole.

Bereft of its power the car would, of course, be immobilized and the lights would go out. Two of the boys would kick the wooden "cow catchers" at either end, slamming them to the tracks. Then the motorman, usually cussing most creatively, would have to descend to street level, deploy the pole again, reset the catchers at the ends and carry on with his trip. Dalhousie campus was a pretty safe sanctuary for the miscreants and we. . .rather, they. . .knew the driver wouldn't abandon his passengers to give chase.

One of the best tram pranks of all was carried out one Halloween night by a group of South End lads who had walked the railway tracks as far as the grain elevators near the waterfront. There the group gathered several pigeons. It was easy to do so by clambering down into the hoppers beneath the railway siding where the grain cars dumped their cargoes. Pigeons would fly into this space and so gorge themselves on the scattered wheat that they could barely fly, making them easy prey for youthful captors. In this instance, it's said, the boys carefully carried off several birds and made them comfortable in the loft of Buddy Gregory's family garage near the Coburg Road railway bridge. There, for a couple of days, they were kept well fed and watered until the evening of the mischief whereupon a cluster of male youths headed up the street, most cosseting a plump urban dove.

At the usual tram stop, the bird-carriers hid in the usual driveway, and a pigeonless boy stood by the curb as the faux passenger. Eventually, a tram arrived and stopped. Another bird-free boy yanked down the trolley pole and the car was frozen in its tracks and pitched into darkness. That's when the rest of the band ran from the driveway, threw the pigeons into the tram's open door and fled with their fellows. Apparently, absolute pandemonium ensued, with the birds flapping about in the pitch black interior of the car messily doing what pigeons do best and making the poor passengers as flustered as the avian invaders. The lark was unusual enough as to be noted in a newspaper story the next day, sporting a subhead something like "Pranksters Cause Tram Commotion." Some of my crowd read it with particular interest.

Soon after my graduation from Queen Elizabeth High School, the doughty old tramcars disappeared, and with them the tracks and the smooth cobblestones in which they were embedded.

The succeeding rubber-tired trolley buses were spacious, fast and silent. But by their advent boys my age had passed the threshold of adolescence, left mischief behind and became the last generation to have grown up with the screech, the smell and the sway of the delightful old Birney cars.

18

Church Days

I DON'T KNOW QUITE WHY I was baptized, catechized and confirmed in the Anglican Church of Canada. My mother had been a Methodist and my father never told me what his denominational background had been before he found his way to Canada after infantry service with the Anzacs in the World War I. But fact is, like my two sisters, I was baptized at King's College Chapel. And that was that.

Our family parish was that of the Cathedral Church of All Saints, several blocks from our home near the Dalhousie campus. My parents had been married there in the tiny St. Stephen's side chapel during the late 1920s. My very earliest recollection of my churchgoing days as a toddler was being terrified by the declamatory speaking style of the clergyman delivering the sermon. Those were the days of stern messages from the pulpit, and I was moved to ask my parents, "Why is the man mad at us?" My childish question was likely delivered less than *sotto voce*, because part of that recollection is hearing titters and chuckles from the closest adults around our pew.

In time I developed an adequate soprano singing voice, and

My sisters Caroline and Jane with their big brother.

was invited to join the Cathedral Boys' Choir. This was no small deal. It meant dressing up in a purple cassock, a gleaming white surplice and a ruffed collar. It meant walking in stately processions every Sunday. It meant weekly practices under an English-accented Ichabod Crane replica named Pew. And, best of all, it meant a monthly salary! Each of us had a locker in the vestry, and on "payday" there would be a small, brown paper envelope placed discreetly on the shelf therein. It was never more than pocket change, but pocket change would buy enough penny candies to make a lad satisfactorily sick.

Between Mr. Pew (often unkindly referred to behind his back as "Pew-de-Doo") and Mr. Montgomery, the ancient organist, we learned the niceties of the so-called Pure White English Sound, a style free from all vulgar, non-Anglican ornamentation. The musical settings of the Eucharist were always by Englishmen such as the Victorian liturgical composer John Stainer. I handled the Stainer arrangements better when lucky enough to be placed beside Walter Fisher in the stalls. Walter, who looked a bit like a teenage version of Humphrey Bogart, was the coolest guy in the choir, and also the best at reading music. With him at my side, I never sang a wrong note.

We also were taught some quirky pronunciations dictated by our musical tutors, particularly in such chanted canticles as the *Magnificat* and the *Nunc Dimittis*, known in choirboy shorthand as "Mag and Nunc." The Mag ended with the words, "Abraham and his seed forever." We were admonished to sing the patriarch's name with no "Abe" and no "Ham" in it. Rather it had to be "Ah-bra-hahm." How very Anglican.

At any rate, there were many things that I enjoyed about choir. There were the surreptitious games of hangman and tic-tac-toe, played with a pencil stub and the back of the Sunday leaflet during the sermon. There were parts of the Cathedral to be explored, including the circular stone steps that reached the roof, then the highest point in the South End (and now dwarfed by subsequent construction). There was the subterranean crypt, certainly the spookiest place in the building. And, by crawling beneath the overhanging oak pulpit, we could spot the tiny carved figure of a church mouse, hidden there by a whimsical craftsman. There were the opportunities to play catch on the adjacent lawn. There was the winter afternoon, after practice, when we pelted Mr. Pew with snowballs from an ambush on Tower Road. And, of course, there was that monthly pay packet.

As time went by and voices changed, I relinquished the role of choirboy and became a member of St Alban's Servers Guild, the group (all male at the time) assigned to such duties as assisting the celebrant with communion, lighting and extinguishing the

Cathedral's many candles or carrying a cross, palm branch, banner or candle in procession.

The Cathedral always had at least three ordained priests as well as the bishop of Nova Scotia, whose beautifully carved throne occupies the chancel. At the time of my membership in the Guild, the clergy included a curate, Rhodes Cooper, a priest assistant, Fr. Frisbee Smith, and the rector, Canon Ellis. It was probably inevitable that we labelled them "Pistol" Cooper, "Machine Gun" Smith and "Cannon" Ellis. The latter was an Englishman with a head that looked like a giant lima bean, its sparse dark hair parted in the middle and plastered flat to the skull with some kind of shiny pomade. He was noted among the lads for his plummy English accent and his stunning lack of a sense of humour. Both these elements figured in the mortifying episode that follows.

One afternoon, the servers were assembled in the choir vestry for some sort of meeting with Canon Ellis. I headed for the opposite side of the cathedral to the clergy vestry on a now-forgotten errand, and decided to go there via a passage behind the carved oaken screen at the back of the altar. Just before I returned to the choir vestry by the same route, Canon Ellis came in and joined me in heading for the meeting. We proceeded along the back wall of the church, but when we got to the door to the vestry, it was closed and locked. As became apparent later, the prankish plan of my peers was to lock both ends of the passage and confine me in there. As Canon Ellis tried the door and rattled the knob to no avail, laughter emerged from the other side. The Canon was not amused. "I say, open this door at once!" he barked. The laughter increased, and one voice shouted gleefully, "Come on, Bennet. We know it's you. Don't try to pretend you're Ellis! You don't sound anything like the old (vulgarity)!"

So there I was, trapped behind a stout oak door in an ill-lit passageway at the back of a massive cathedral beside an enraged, lima-beaned cleric with pasted-down hair. His normally pale face was growing purple, and his feet were doing an agitated little dance beneath his cassock as he roared once more, "I say! Open this door!" Slowly, the laughter died as my compatriots began to realize the admonition was indeed issued by the real rector and not by their intended target. The door was unlocked, and the rector and I entered a room full of blushing adolescents, some examining the ceiling, some the floor and some their fingernails. There followed an eloquent tirade by the infuriated priest, ending with an explicit dismissal from the vestry, the cathedral and, if I remember rightly, the face of the earth.

If clerical anger was one aspect of life as an altar boy, there was also the majesty of participation in the high theatre of the sung high Eucharist and the comforting drone of prayers at Matins and Evensong, both of which have almost disappeared from Anglican practice. And on assigned weekday mornings, especially in winter, there was the tiresome chore of trudging alone through dark streets to serve at early communion in the chapel where my parents had been wed. Sometimes it would just be the celebrant and oneself in attendance. Sometimes there would be a white-haired parishioner or two in attendance mumbling the responses along with the server. There was no musical majesty involved, just the droning voice of the celebrant. But the rich language of the *Book of Common Prayer* was music to the ears of a word-struck kid. It still is.

As for the now-departed Canon Ellis, I can easily imagine him hammering at St. Peter's pearly portal, indignantly braying, "I say! Open this door!"

19

High School

I entered grade ten at Queen Elizabeth High School with a huge sense of excitement. After all, the school was scarcely five years old and quite unlike any of the other school buildings in Halifax, especially the mouldy old LeMarchant Street ark. A gymnasium, auditorium and extra wings would eventually be added years later, but my mates and I were sufficiently impressed by the school's original conformation. Rather than peeling paint and sagging floors, we were surrounded by gleaming, ultramodern materials laid out in a clean and (to us) radical style. There were electric bells for class changes, a public address system and new-fangled, draft-free windows. Everything smelled new, rather than musty. There was even a touch of art deco ornamentation around the main entrance. And the building was surrounded not by gritty cinders and hardpan, but real grass. And how grown-up I felt amid students who shaved, some who even drove cars and motorcycles, girls who looked like glamour queens, a chemistry lab with beakers and Bunsen burners and a school office with a full-time secretary. This was indeed the big time.

Our principal was the awe-inspiring Ralph E. Marshall, a

small, grizzled man with a large reputation known to students (except to his face) as "R.E." Nobody messed with R.E., and my one encounter with him (detailed later) stands out in my memory as the most terrifying and embarrassing moment of my school life. The teachers were mostly veterans of the city grade schools or the venerable Halifax County Academy at Brunswick and Sackville. A few were veterans of another sort, recently de-mobbed servicemen and women who'd been through the war. As with grade school they ranged, in my experience, from kindly to comic to ineffectual to able and dedicated.

Unlike our previous schooldays, we wandered from class to class for subjects other than that proffered by our homeroom teacher. Classes were designated according to the subject set taken by students, and, as one who took Latin, I went through in C1, B1 and A1 along with a set of classmates that changed little. Along the way, alliances were formed and changed. For instance my long-time neighbourhood pal, Ducker Ross, only took grade ten at QEH and then moved on to Nova Scotia Agricultural School (Aggie) in Debert.

Probably my closest associates from that time on were Jimmy Brown, a star swimmer and trombone player, and Armen Arakelian, whom I'd known as a classmate and fellow altar boy at All Saints Cathedral since about grade five. Both guys were masters of mischief, and I must admit to a similar turn of mind. More thought, creativity and diligence went into our various pranks than into studies. Even without much study, I did well enough in English, History, Social Studies, Languages and other subjects related to the humanities. Unfortunately, I was pretty poor in the sciences and a total wipeout in math. And, sadly, no marks were given out for tomfoolery.

As for the monkey business, I'll recount only a couple of our best tricks, surely worth an A+ in anyone's book. They were the best kind: crafted to leave the culprits undetected because they were self-operating setups. One teacher, who invariably put his briefcase by his desk, had us in his last class of the day and hurriedly departed with it as soon as the bell rang. We sneaked in during lunch period with a length of cord, which we used to tie the briefcase handle to his chair. Class passed uneventfully until the bell rang and our victim stated, "Class dismissed," grabbed the briefcase and strode toward the door. We'd allowed enough slack for him to take a stride or two before the line tightened, and when it did the stunt was very satisfactory. His arm jerked backward, and he found himself dragging his overturned chair behind him. His baffled reaction was right out of a vaudeville act, and the whole class erupted into laughter which went unshared by the butt of the prank, a humourless man at the best of times.

We caught another creature of habit in an even more dramatic way. This teacher, we observed, began his class by pulling open the deep drawer on the left hand side of his desk, and withdrawing his notes. I think it was Armen who had the initial inspiration, and it was beautiful. One lunch hour, we three went to the Halifax Public Gardens, just a block or so from school. There we captured a pigeon and carried it with care back to QEH.

You can probably see this one coming. Before class, into that soon-to-be-opened drawer went Mr. Pigeon, and we perpetrators took our seats as the room began to fill. Armen and Jimmy and I sat as nonchalantly as possible until the crucial moment came and the teacher arrived, sat down and grabbed the handle of the deep drawer. Wings flapped, feathers flew, teacher recoiled. Girls squealed, class laughed. A four-star success, and (till now, long after statutory limitations have expired) untraceable!

My one encounter with the principal was not due to a surreptitious prank, but to an overt and inexcusable one. One of our math teachers was sadly unable to impose discipline in her class, which led to rampant disrespect on the part of many male oafs in the class, me included. The incident began when this poor soul noticed me out of my seat and querulously directed me to return to it. Playing to the gallery, I committed a major act of insolence, saying something like, "Yeah, yeah, I'll be right with you."

The reaction, a beat and a half later, was not titter from the class or a chiding from the gentle teacher. It came from the stentorian larynx of an onlooker who had entered the room via the rear door, unnoticed. It was Mr. Marshall himself. He roared, literally roared, one thunderous syllable: "HOY!" I jumped as though a bomb had gone off in my back pocket. Heart pounding and head swimming, I made it back to my desk and sat trembling. R.E. was beside me instantly, his rage manifest. I would have preferred the Seventh Circle of Hell to my seat in that classroom. I was seriously afraid that the furious man might lay hands on me and shake me into a coma. My face crimson, I fixed a blurry gaze on the desktop and waited. When it came, the reproof was worse than anything I might have imagined.

"Bennet," shouted the principal, "you are anything but a gentleman." That was bad. But worse was to come, as he added, "And I blush to think that you are the son of one."

The reference to my father, a well-known and widely admired professor and schoolbook editor, was like a hardwood stake to the heart. R.E. turned on his heel and was gone, leaving a palpable silence in the room. My prayers that the crust of the earth should open and swallow me into complete oblivion were unanswered. I have no memory of the rest of that particular Math period, but no few seconds of my many years stand out more strongly in my memory today.

I must recount another small escapade that was carried out by (and backfired on) another friend, Ramsay Keillor. Ramsay was an incorrigible cut-up and an excellent mimic. One day, as we sat in the sloping seats of the room where physics was taught we began to realize that the teacher, one Otto Fritze, was late for class. As more time went by, Ramsay saw his opportunity and went to the front of the room and began a hilarious imitation of Mr. Fritze: the voice, the mannerisms and the pet phrases right on the mark. As Ramsay warmed to his task, the classroom door opened quietly and in crept Mr. Fritze, with his finger to his lips. He stood slightly behind his imitator and off to one side, folded his arms and listened with the rest of us. Eventually Ramsay perceived that the eyes of the class were no longer on him, but slightly stage left. When his eyes met those of his subject, it provided a double take worthy of the glory days of vaudeville. And that classic double take is where my memory of the occasion ends, though it would have been typical of Mr. Fritze to have merely sent the crestfallen Ramsay back to his seat.

I became co-editor of the school newspaper, *Beth's News and Views*, along with my neighbourhood friend David "Gumpy" Anderson. It consisted of gossip ("What cute blonde in B-7 has her eye on a certain hockey goalie?") to editorial ("Student Apathy Hits New Low at QEH") to shocking ("Drinking on Train Mars Kentville Hockey Trip"). There were scratchy cartoons, sports scores and the like, the whole melange printed in smeared and blotchy fashion on the school mimeograph machine. Gumpy insisted on our signing off each issue with the phrase "So long, coolies." All in all, a perfectly typical piece of student garbage journalism.

As with grade school, the hymn singing went on, but now with the added impetus of being broadcast on the PA system. It was "led" by a motley six or eight of us who gathered around a microphone at the beginning of the school day in the office. Again it made me wonder what schoolmates like Bert Whitzman, Saul Garson and Ed Rubin were doing in their respective home rooms (and minds) as this went on. Armen, my partner in the two-boy bass section, kept me constantly on the edge of trouble, singing wicked parodies of the hymn lyrics in my right ear, not quite loud enough to be picked up by the microphone.

Music and dancing featured strongly in the Halifax high school scene in my day. There was Twixteen, a dance club on Hollis Street and HI-Y, a Friday evening dance at the YMCA. Another teen dance club in the North End was Capers Junction.

Commercially operated dance halls included the Jubilee Boat Club (known to all as "the Jube") and the Olympic Gardens on Cunard Street. Sometimes we danced to real live bands, most of them so-called tenor bands featuring three tenor saxes and one trumpet, piano, bass and drums. There was a pretty good choice: Jerry Naugler, Arne Benson, "Jit" Cunningham, Joe Laba, Les Single and others leaders got gigs aplenty.

The dancing itself was fairly sedate, but at least offered a welcome opportunity to hold a partner close and do some serious nuzzling. Jive was still at its crest, and at first I thought all it involved was uncontrolled jumping about, which must have made me a ridiculous figure on the floor and an embarrassment to my partners. I soon enough caught on that jitterbugging was a very skilled and well-controlled dance form, and retreated to the sidelines to watch the likes of Donnie Cooley and his girlfriend Mary demonstrate how it should be done. Which was coolly.

I don't remember dress for social occasions being any different from school wear. At QEH, there was a code, unwritten but strictly adhered to. The girls wore seemly skirts and sweaters to school, the boys shirts, ties and sports jackets. My only "fashion statement" was a particularly horrendous tie featuring a purple, puce and chartreuse floral pattern, worn for its shocking effect. Playing to the gallery again. The really edgy guys were the ones who affected ducktail haircuts and peg pants, or "drapes," featuring pleats at the waist and ballooning knees that tapered to a tight, sixteen-inch cuff. These had a slightly outlaw touch to them, and none of my crowd would have been allowed out of the house in them.

The absolute standard for high-tone gentleman's wear at QEH was set by Mr. Len Hannon ("Gus" to us when out of earshot). He was my home room and Latin teacher in grade twelve, and was a fashion plate who would have turned admiring heads at in any boardroom on the continent. He wore knife-edge creases in his trousers, gleaming white shirts with starched collars and just an inch of cuff showing at his wrists. There was a time some years back when restaurants would keep ties available for customers who appeared without one. Well, "Gus" was way ahead of them. He kept an assortment of ties in a desk drawer ready for any lad who dared show up without one.

I'll never forget the afternoon some of us from his class attended a Halifax and District Baseball League game at the Wanderers Grounds after school. Mr. Hannon was perched on the bleachers a few seats away from us, impeccable as always. And there on the diamond, in his Halifax Capitals uniform was his brother Billy, who was something of a sporting legend at that time, both in baseball and as a hockey star with the Sydney Millionaires. Like his

Mr. Hannon's dress code.

rumpled, tobacco-chewing colleagues, Billy Hannon was far from chic. But his dapper brother Len was the most enthusiastic fan at the field that day, and we (knowing little or nothing about baseball) took our cues from him, cheering wildly whenever he clapped.

In sum, if there was one outstanding teacher at the QEH of my time, it was "Gus" Hannon. He was not to be trifled with, but always fair. The respect he commanded is legendary, extending through his own twenty-year period as principal some years later. His was the last Latin class I ever passed, and our graduation ceremony in the spring of 1949 the last I took part in. It was held at the Dalhousie Gymnasium, QEH being still without an auditorium, and the speaker was the Mayor of Halifax, J.E. Ahern. A newspaper sportswriter by trade, he spoke with pride of the plans for building a new "gymanasium" at QEH for the use of school "athaletes."

A year later I sat in that same Dalhousie gym for final exams in my freshman year. Without Len Hannon's guidance, my Latin mark was as disastrous as my math, and my formal education came to its close.

Just as an epilogue, I should mention the fact that (at the age of seventy) I had a hip replacement at the QEII Health Centre, a stone's throw from my old high school. My recovery took longer than anticipated, and as I lay bored to death in my hospital bed, a visitor knocked and entered. It was, of all people, Mr. Hannon, well into his nineties, come to see how the erstwhile occupant of the front desk in the second row, Class of '49, was doing.

We had a lovely chat, but I wish I'd had the presence of mind to greet him with "De gustibus non est disputandum," or some other remnant of his teachings.

20

Characters

IN THE TIME COVERED BY this memoir, most everybody shared a knowledge of who the town characters were. Among the best known was a man who stood at the then epicentre of town, the intersection of Sackville and Barrington. He was Hector MacLeod, a robust policeman in a uniform augmented by white gloves, a white-crowned cap and a gleaming whistle on a lanyard. Believe it or not, when I was young there were no traffic lights anywhere in town. What we did have was Hec MacLeod. His intersection was at that time the Hollywood and Vine, the Portage and Main, the Broadway & 42nd Street of Halifax. It was surrounded by retail stores, office buildings, lunch counters and the city's two five and dime stores, Woolworth's and the Metropolitan.

MacLeod was eventually replaced by another traffic controller, Syd Clarke, a well-known hockey player who became even better known for his presence at Sackville and Barrington. As I recall, Clarke wore standard police kit, minus the white accessories used by Hector.

Along Barrington Street, two blocks north or south of the

main intersection, one would often encounter a short, dumpy man who dressed rather shabbily and walked without swinging his arms. He never seemed to catch anyone's eye: his gaze stayed permanently on the sidewalk ahead of his feet. And, at least to my boyish set, he bore no name other than the Millionaire. This title was conferred because he was reputed to be rich beyond the dreams of avarice. It was always a kick to be with someone who didn't know the legend, and be able to say, "Psst! See that guy over there? He's a multimillionaire. Never know it, would you?"

Between the Metropolitan Store and Woolworth's on the ground floor of the Roy Building there sat another familiar figure. He was a blind accordionist, quite a good looking, well-groomed fellow with a big Hohner 120 bass instrument. There was a tin cup affixed to the frame that contained a dozen or so pencils. These were ostensibly for sale, though I never saw anyone take one. I rather imagine he ended his career with the same few Dixon HBs he started with. In reality, he was a professional busker, rather than a pencil salesman, and a quite adept player at that. But he was known to any Haligonian who ever came downtown, and favoured with a coin or two by hundreds every day.

In one of the two five and dime stores behind him (the Met, as I recall), laboured another cherished Halifax character, "Knucker" Burns. Knucker was a smallish, cherubic fellow with no further use for dentists. Gumming a damp cigar butt, he swept the floors and did other odd jobs around the store. The sight of a pretty girl always elicited the same response from Knucker: a delighted, "Hello, dear!" with the second word of the phrase long drawn out. Knucker was a rabid sports fan, and had been adopted by the whole sporting set of Halifax, appearing to great acclaim at hockey and ball games. He was apparently a big Boston fan,

Sackville and Barrington streets: the centre of the universe.

because I well remember one winter when the canteen at the
old Shirley Street Arena bore a slot-topped box with the message

"Send Knucker to Boston." If the eventual dirty, bulging state of the box meant anything, Halifax fans were generous with their coinage and, I hope, did indeed pay Knucker's expenses for an excursion to Beantown to root for the Bruins.

While perhaps not as widely known to the general population as some town characters, a very small man named Buster was certainly familiar to South End boys who, attracted by the shiny equipment, liked to drop into the Morris Street Fire Station at the corner of Robie. We were usually welcomed, sometimes just tolerated but seldom sent packing. I particularly recall one time when we were ushered upstairs to the living quarters and allowed to slide down the gleaming brass pole to the ground floor.

Any visit to the station was likely to feature Buster, who was a resident of the City Home on the adjoining property. His mental capacity was insufficient to allow gainful employment, but on the other hand he had a huge ability to enjoy himself. As an adoptee of the smoke-eaters, he reported to the station every day dressed in a uniform they'd provided, cut down to fit his four feet and a bit and topped with a regulation cap. Buster took his "duties" very seriously, doing a bit of sweeping or polishing here and there. I used to reflect on how much better his life had been made by the firemen, given that many other poor souls from the City Home enjoyed no more activity than a daily supervised walk, round and round in a circle, on a fenced-off part of the grounds.

Then there was the seller of the *Daily Star* whose corner was Queen and Spring Garden, known by one and all. The *Herald-Mail* and *Chronicle-Star* were separate journals at the time, and this man carried an amazing number of papers, probably weighing some fifty or sixty pounds when both his bags were full. Bearing this weight over the years had given him a permanent slump. He had a slight hesitation in his speech, and every passerby got a lop-sided smile and a droned, "St-star, lady?" or "St-star, sir?"

More often seen on the tramcars than the sidewalk was a man I'll call only Mr. M, in deference to any surviving relatives. Mr. M, the story went, had been an outstanding champion golfer whose zeal for strong drink had given him what was then (and may be still) called "wet brain." Whatever the cause, the effect was remarkable. Mr. M would sit with one hand along the back of his seat, while flapping the other in a way that brought the fingers together with a sound like a pistol shot: much louder than a mere snap. We boys all had tried to emulate the motion to no avail. This was Mr. M's particular and unmatchable skill. His other trademark was a kind of unintelligible mumbling that would suddenly rise to a growl, then a roar, filling the car with its resonance. Most people knew Mr. M by both name and habit, meaning that he usually had a seat to himself. It was also widely known that he was quite harmless, living inside his own booze-bombarded head and addressing only his personal devils. But there were those whose unawareness made them vulnerable, and the real fun for any schoolboys on board was what happened when the car was nearly full and someone (preferably a South End matron) boarded and unwittingly sat down beside Mr. M. There might be an uneventful moment or two before Mr. M sprang into action: "Aaarggh! Yahh! Grarrh! Snap! Pow! Ugga-bugga!" And the seatmate would decamp in terror and confusion, to a fugue of snorts and giggles from any raffish youngsters lucky enough to witness the scene.

There were others, perhaps less well-known, who still affirm the contention that the Halifax of my childhood had a small town quality when it came to recognizable characters. Among these minor figures was "Rushing Rhoda" (my patent name for her), a lady whose beat was usually Spring Garden Road. This middle-aged woman had her own version of what Boy Scouts called "scout's pace": twenty steps walking, twenty running. I don't believe she actually counted, but if you watched her for more than about ten seconds, you'd see her change from a fast walk to a trot and back again. Probably some form of compulsive behaviour, and certainly a harmless one.

There was also the Lady With No Nose, the site of whose missing feature was covered by a two-inch veil of lace. There was much horrified speculation as to the cause of her misfortune, but it would probably be wise to refrain from discussing them. And, to round out the cast, we had a guy who strode the streets in a strange combination of Highland dress, some military, some civilian, all well past its expiry date. The wearer, too, looked like hygiene might not have been his strong suit. But with his massive walrus moustache and swinging kilt, he turned many the head downtown.

All these personalities have since disappeared, but the town was once a richer place for them. And Halifax has become richer yet in so many ways: the North Commons is now a grassy expanse of recreation space, the Central Library is a world-class trophy and the waterfront a shared treasure. Also, the municipality now embraces Dartmouth, Bedford and much of the surrounding countryside and is home to about 40 per cent of all Nova Scotians. I hope that some of them have found enjoyment and edification in the memories of an aged but proud Haligonian.

Photo Credits